TRAVEL SOLO

Eliza Croft

GIRLS WHO

THE ESSENTIAL GUIDE
FOR FIRST TIME
TRAVEL ADVENTURERS

WHO

TRAVEL

SOLO

CONTENTS

INTRODUCTION

Where do I even start? Like most people who have ever thought about exploring the world, I was overwhelmed, nervous and terrified of the unknown. What if I got lonely or homesick? Was I capable of doing this by myself?

Before setting off on your travels, you may have some of these thoughts, unanswered questions, fears and worries compounding in your mind. Planning your first ever solo trip can be scary, but it's also extremely exciting. You don't know where to start, you don't know what to expect or how you're going to feel, but one thing all first-time solo travellers have in common is—none of us have a clue what we're doing! We all feel a call to something more, something greater, something beyond the ordinary.

If you've ever thought about going travelling, which you most likely have if you're reading this book—unless you're my friends and family who are just reading to support me (I appreciate you all)—then look no further: I aim to provide you with everything you need to know about travelling solo as a female, so that you feel prepared, confident and excited about finally taking the leap. I'll discuss all the many trial-tested mistakes I made and tell you how you can avoid doing the same, but I'll also show you that it's totally fine to mess up a few times. It's all part of the journey and the only way we learn is by making mistakes and trying again (or reading this book on how to avoid them!)

So, you may be wondering who I am, or who am I to be writing a book about female solo travel? At the time of publishing this book, I'm 23 years old, I've travelled to 27 countries, a number of them on solo trips. The majority of countries I've travelled to alone have been in South East Asia. I lived in Indonesia for eight months and I've recently based myself in Thailand. For how long? Who knows? The only thing I know for sure is that there's still a lot of the world I want to see before I settle in one place. That's if I ever decide to settle. Solo travel has provided me with a lot of lessons that I wish I'd known before I started travelling, and that's why I'm about to share all of my knowledge with you.

My experience in solo travel has allowed me to find something I love to do, which is to inspire others to solo travel. I believe this is what I'm supposed to be doing, at least at this point in my life. There are two things that have had a huge positive impact on my life, which are solo travelling and self-development. I decided to combine my love for books and my knowledge of solo travel into one. I started to receive messages asking for advice and help with travel. But it was a challenge to give detailed answers in a single Instagram message, so I decided to write a short e-book in which I offered a few tips on where to start when planning a solo trip.

I told a friend I had met while travelling that my e-book was almost finished and he told me to carry on writing to turn my little project into a 'real' book. At first, I didn't believe that I could produce more than I had already written. 10,000 words seemed like a lot and I didn't think I had anything else left to say that I could use to incorporate into an actual book. I was also worried that I was *too young* to write a book, and that people would wonder what experience a 23-year-old girl could possibly have. But when I told my friend about my concerns, he immediately changed my perspective. Meeting people like this friend is one of the main reasons I love to travel. You will meet other solo travellers who want to see you succeed—people who push you to achieve your highest potential. Without this friend saying to me, "You should carry on writing," I wouldn't have written this book. I wouldn't have challenged my abilities and proved to myself what I'm capable of.

I loved writing when I was a child. I wrote letters to my grandma. I sat on the sofa in my nana's house and wrote long stories while I waited for her to cook me some chicken nuggets and potato smiley faces. I always knew that one day I would write a book, but I imagined that to happen when I was at least thirty years old. Now I realise, there's no timeline on life. We don't have to wait until we're thirty to write a book. We don't have to have children and buy a house by a certain age. We don't have to go to university as soon as we leave school and we don't have to have our whole life figured out in our twenties. We can do all these things whenever we feel like the time is right for us, that's if we even want these things at all. I feel truly blessed to be combining my love for reading, writing, travel and helping others all into one way of life.

Not to sound cliché, but travel has changed my life in so many ways. I travelled solo for the first time in 2019 when I was twenty years old; I sat on the plane to Hong Kong and looked out of the plane window, I thought to myself, 'Sh*t, what have I done?' At the time I didn't know that this would be the trip that would change the direction of my life forever. On this first trip, I travelled to Indonesia, Australia and Vietnam. I'd never done anything like this before. I had always been a timid person. I didn't know what I wanted in life. There was one thing I knew for sure though, I loved adventure and the rush of adrenaline.

Growing up, I loved playing hide and seek with my cousins and siblings, in our pitch-black garden and during our family camping and surfing trips to Cornwall. I loved fun trips out to waterparks with my cousins. One cousin in particular (you know who you are), would persuade the five of us to run past the lifeguard and sneak down the slides all at the same time (we got many warnings for this, but it was good for the adrenaline rush). Every year, I looked forward to an annual camping trip with around twenty school friends on an open field. No matter the weather, we would always make it memorable.

I had an amazing childhood that I'm extremely grateful for. I never realised at the time how much I craved adventure, but I jumped at any chance of exploration.

For the last few years, although I had been *averagely* happy, I'd felt disconnected, uncertain and lost. Something was missing. I realised I was living a very mediocre life. I had an average job. I was in an average long-term relationship. My overall day-to-day life felt average. None of those things were bad. I learnt a lot from each of them and I needed to go through those few mediocre years of my life to come to the realisation that I craved more than that. I craved adventure and freedom. Those were, and still are, my greatest values. One of my biggest fears was the fear of wasting time. I didn't want to live my life without *living* my life.

I remember a time when my ex-boyfriend showed me a photo of a house he'd been looking at. He wanted us to move in together. The expression on my face was a picture, to say the least. The photo gave me nightmares. It also gave me a huge realisation that settling down was 110% not what I wanted for probably the next ten years of my life. Buying a house was hardly one of my main needs. I wanted to explore the world and build up some unforgettable experiences.

After seeing the dreaded photo of the potential house, I ran as far away as possible from anything that had 'security' or 'settle down' written over it (7819.94 miles away, to be exact). I left my job. I left my relationship. And I left the country that I'd grown up in.

The relationship I speak about had been going on for four years. At first, it was great. It was everything my teenage-self had dreamt of; he treated me well and smothered me with thoughtful surprises, dates and attention. Two years into the relationship, I decided I wanted to travel, but he didn't want to join me. Travel didn't interest him. I decided to travel alone.

When I booked this trip, things started to change within the relationship. Although we had spoken about my decision beforehand and he ensured me he was happy (not that this should have altered my decision either way), I noticed an immediate alteration in the way I was feeling. I felt guilt in a way I'd never felt before, so much so that I only travelled for one month because I felt pressured to come home to him. I understood why he felt the way he did about me travelling; he didn't know the people I would meet. He didn't know I'd be safe and he knew he would miss me being around. Unfortunately, we hardly spoke throughout my trip. I had the trip of a lifetime and I felt like I had to apologise for that.

My mental health started to decline and I was experiencing frequent anxiety attacks. I felt a huge weight on top of me. I felt trapped in my job, in my relationship and in my own anxious mind. I missed travel and I was feeling desperate to get out of the country. I decided I wanted to move to Indonesia.

I explained this to my partner, who understandably wasn't happy about my decision. However, he soon warmed to the idea of joining me when he realized I was going to move away regardless of whether he came with me or not.

After I handed my notice in at my job, I started to notice that this wasn't what he wanted. He wasn't doing this because he wanted to travel and experience a different lifestyle. He was doing this because he was worried about being alone. I knew his main values were security and comfort. That's what he'd get from staying in his good job and settling down with someone in the comfort of his hometown, not from not having a stable income and moving to the other side of the world with a girl who craved a change in location every few months.

Knowing someone was relying on me for their happiness placed a lot of pressure on me, so I decided I was going to make the move alone. I ended the relationship, which wasn't an easy process, as most breakups aren't. I left for Bali. Getting to where I am now required a lot of reflection work, therapy sessions and self-discovery. I don't think I could have chosen a better island to heal; I was surrounded by inspiring, powerful people, scenery that made me grateful for every day and a lifestyle that promised complete freedom.

The fear of settling for a life I didn't want scared me more than leaving my comforts behind to follow my dream of travelling. People don't change until not changing is the less comfortable option and this was exactly the case for me. As well as that, I physically didn't have any more energy to give to anything that didn't resonate with me. I found that if you started putting energy into things that aligned with somebody else's vision instead of your own, you quickly burned out. Avoid being a people-pleaser, you have the capability to carve your own path to success, whatever that might look like.

Speaking of people-pleasers, I used to be a huge one myself. Before I first went travelling, I was riddled with guilt about leaving my family behind. I knew that my mum constantly worried every time I was abroad on my own (although she should be getting used to that by now). I knew that my dogs would have no idea where I'd disappeared to. I thought that my workplace wouldn't be able to cope without me, which is what they'd told me to make me stick around a little longer, and I knew that my nana was unable to visit, so the only way I'd be able to keep in touch was through FaceTime. As most of you might know from life during the pandemic, teaching your grandparents how to use technology can be somewhat challenging, to say the least.

You will most likely experience the feeling of guilt from leaving loved ones behind for a while, but remember that these people have your best interests at heart. They want you to follow your dreams and desires. They want you to experience new things in life and they will support you in doing that. If they don't show support, you should ask yourself why they're holding you back from doing something that you have your heart set on. Do you need their permission to go? Do you need to take a step back from them? Once you go, the feeling of guilt decreases and everyone realises that you being away from home for a while isn't so bad after all.

I'd always loved the idea of travelling the world. When I was growing up, I was intrigued when listening to my auntie's stories of all the amazing places she'd been to and the experiences she'd had. My auntie visited many different countries and this was an inspiration to me. It showed me that living a different kind of life was possible. At the time I had the realisation that I could actually go travelling instead of just thinking about it, I was working in an office in a customer advisor role five days a week. I knew there had to be more to life than this and what better time to travel than when you have no idea what you're doing with your life? I realised that I had the power to create my own story. I decided I would figure it out as I went and I trusted that I was capable. So, I booked a one-way ticket and flew to the other side of the world. Well, it wasn't as simple as that, but that's pretty much how it went.

Since then, I've watched my life rapidly develop into something beautiful, something I'm proud of and something I'm extremely grateful for. I'm now obsessed with my life and I feel truly blessed to be living it.

Travelling solo taught me more about myself, about others and the world around me than any type of school education ever had.

Travel gave me real-life education.

Travelling Solo will teach you to observe the world around you and to see the value in the little things. It teaches you more, gives you more, and makes you believe that *you* are more.

You will have probably heard the saying 'You travel to find yourself'—this phrase is not wrong, but rather than finding yourself, I believe travel helps you to *create* yourself and create the life you desire. It will push you out of your comfort zone, make you question what you want out of life and it will challenge you in more ways than imaginable. But you will be inspired by the people you meet, stunned by the beautiful world we live in and addicted to the adrenaline that solo travel gives to you.

You have the capability to carve your own path to success, whatever that might look like.

GETTING STARTED

Have a burning desire to see the world but no idea where to start? This chapter will guide you into taking the first step—making a decision.

Unfortunately, nobody can tell you where the best place to travel is, everyone is different and it all comes down to personal preference. But here are a few questions designed to help you choose the right destination/s for yourself. Write your answers down as this will give your mind more openness and clarity.

- ❖ Are there any countries you've always wanted to go to?
- ❖ When you think of travelling, what is the first place that comes to mind?
- ❖ Do you prefer hot weather, a cooler climate or some-where with lots of snow?
- ❖ Do you prefer island life or a busy city?
- ❖ Do you plan on relaxing or will you want to be exploring?
- ❖ Do you plan on travelling to new places or do you want to stick to one area?
- ❖ Do you want time alone or to be surrounded by new people?
- ❖ Do you want to learn a specific skill or try a new hobby?

Once you've considered these questions, you should have some places in mind that stand out. All you have to do now is make the decision on which place you're going to choose.

After you've made your decision, it's time to get stuck into the research. You can use blogs, YouTube, Instagram hashtags and locations to find out more about your chosen country and the best places to visit, or you can reach out to people who have already been and ask for their recommendations.

The last and most difficult part is planning. If you plan to travel around several different places, I recommend searching for ready-made travel itineraries for your desired country. For example, if I search for an itinerary for Thailand and go onto the images section on Google, it will show maps of different ways to travel around Thailand. You can research these specific areas and decide which you'd like to go to. The itinerary is a guide on what is the best way to get around. I usually look at websites of tour companies as they are likely to have the best planned-out itineraries for the most efficient and cost-effective routes. You could even follow their itinerary and add in any extra stops or take out places you don't fancy. Once you've found some places you like the look of, you can pinpoint these on the Google Maps app to make it easier to plan your route. Lonely Planet guides are also a great investment when you're planning your travels—they are full of expert advice and guidance and there is information about every country.

◼ **Be strategic with your planning and make sure you choose your destination with intent; what is the reason you want to go there?**

If you find yourself procrastinating when it comes to research and planning, you should set some time in your calendar to do this, otherwise, before you know it, weeks will have gone by, then months, and you're still in the exact same place as when you started.

My friend recently told me a story which went something like this: A man asked a woman what her main priority was and she said that it was writing her book. He then asked her if she was working on this every day and she said no because she had got other jobs to do around the house, she needed to look after her children and she had other work commitments. He said, "But if writing your book is your main priority in life, you should be working on this every single day." We should never be so busy that we don't have time to work on the things that are important to us.

If travelling is your priority at this point in your life, if it's the thing that you're desperate to go and experience, then you should prioritise working on this every single day. Research, plan, save your money, take action and book the flight. Change doesn't come to those who sit around and wait. It comes to those who take actionable steps to make it happen. So, take the first step, sit down and write down your answers to the questions above. Try not to look at how much needs to be done overall. Just focus on the next step that needs to be taken.

For many types of solo trips, you won't need to plan as much as you think you do. If you're travelling alone and you are keen to meet new people, it's better to be flexible with plans, in case opportunities arise when you meet new groups of people. You don't want to overbook yourself and then miss out on a trip with your new friends because your travel schedule is already fully planned. If you're like me—I prefer to 'wing it' when I'm solo travelling—then all you *really* need to have pre-booked is your first few nights' accommodation, because after travelling long hours, you want to be stress-free and know that you have a place to stay when you arrive. If you're only travelling for a short amount of time, book activities, accommodation and your return flight in advance because you're not going to be as flexible as you would be if you were travelling for a longer period.

Once you've decided where to go and planned out a basic itinerary, you're well on your way to making your travel dream a reality. So, let's get into it!

Change doesn't come to those who sit around and wait. It comes to those who take actionable steps to make it happen.

@elizacroft_

DEVELOPING THE
ADVENTURER'S MINDSET

You are decided. You're going. And then, suddenly, your limiting beliefs, worries, and fears start to creep in. It's a normal human response. What do you do? This is your time to embrace what I call the **Adventurer's Mindset**.

One of the biggest limiting beliefs I hear about is the fear of other people's opinions.

"What will my boss think of me if I leave this job?"
"I could never travel; I'll feel too guilty leaving my family."
"What if people judge me?"

Whether it's your family, friends, work colleagues or strangers, nothing anyone else has to say should hold you back. Other people will try to put you off big ideas because it's not something they would do themselves, which is a reflection of their own insecurities. I like to always look at it as having tunnel vision; once you decide what you want, don't look anywhere else other than where you're going. The people who support you and tell you to go and live your dream are the people you need to surround yourself with (virtually, while you're travelling of course).

It might be difficult for loved ones to hear you're thinking of going away for a while, most commonly partners or parents. Everyone will react and understand your decision differently. You should reassure them, sit down with them and explain what you're planning to do. You could plan out your conversation beforehand if you think certain loved ones will try to talk you out of it. You have to be prepared to deal with their reactions and give them time to come around to the idea. Not everyone will experience this, you may be lucky and have good feedback from everyone you tell, but just be aware that you may have to reassure some more than others.

Travelling solo as a woman is a bold choice. Many others have done it and you can too. Freya Stark for example, took a huge risk on her first trip to Lebanon in 1927. She crossed the border illegally and in secret, as travel was not allowed in the region. She travelled during the night and was caught by French army officers. Stark later discovered that her capture by the police was a fortunate escape as she was being followed by murderers, determined to kill the woman wandering around the area alone. People wanted to know how she survived in the wilderness surrounded by bandits.

Of course, your risk to travel solo will (hopefully) not include illegal activities like Stark's, but your solo trip will take courage. You'll have to take risks and overcome challenges the same way she did.

It's extremely common for people to make comments about anything new you try.

I had people say, "But why would you want to live in a third-world country?" "Bali looks sh*t, I much prefer the U.K," "How are you going to survive on your own?" "You're the last person I'd imagine to be able to travel alone," "You're just running away."

Comments like these will plant doubts in your head and make you question whether you're capable of travelling solo and that's when you'll start to think, 'maybe it's safer to just stay where I am'.

But really, there is no greater danger than staying where you are. How will you ever grow? How will you build experiences? How will you know what things genuinely light you up? I'm a firm believer in being present in the moment and being grateful for what I already have. You need to find happiness within yourself, so that you can feel it wherever you are in the world.

Ask yourself these questions: Are you staying where you are because you're truly happy with where your life is at right now? Or are you staying where you are because you're afraid of uncertainty, afraid of trying something new or afraid of being uncomfortable? Think about it.

As well as the doubtful comments, you'll also receive a shower of positive and uplifting comments which will outweigh the negative.

"You're so brave."
"You're such an inspiration."
"Go and live your dream."
"I'm so proud of you."

These are the type of comments from people who see you're worthy enough, brave enough and more than capable to do this.

We are brought up to think we have to go to school, get a university degree and then work a corporate job for 40+ years of our lives. When we're brought up to believe in these 'societal norms', it's difficult to see what's really possible these days with the different, new tools we have at our fingertips. Wanting something different in life to what the majority of society wants is totally fine; it's good to be different. That being said, it's also fine if you want to follow society's norms. It all comes down to what values matter most to you personally. Just remember, you are the only person who has to wake up every day and live your life, so why not live it the way you've always dreamed of? Follow your inner guidance and live a life that is true to yourself and not to what others expect from you.

So now for what I'd say is probably my biggest piece of travel advice—◨ **Do not wait for other people to travel with you!**

Honestly, if you're waiting on other people to travel with you, you'll never end up going. Your friends or partner might seem keen to go with you at first, but then the excuses start to come in and you're left waiting around for months, or even years. If the time is right for you, don't wait around, go solo! You can always go again later on down the line when your friend or partner is ready to go too.

I understand leaving people behind to go travelling, especially your partner, can be upsetting. I've done this myself more than once now, but I can say those were the best decisions I ever made. If you have that burning desire to travel, but you end up not going because your partner didn't want to go with you, you'll only end up resenting them years down the line and travelling will remain a dream to you. You deserve the life you most genuinely want, not the life somebody else wants for you.

'That could never be me.'—When you look at other travellers on social media and think you could never have their life, those thoughts always come down to not feeling good enough. But let me ask you, why do you feel like you don't deserve this? Why aren't you good enough? Absolutely everybody in this world deserves to experience travel if that's what they want to do. You deserve to see this beautiful world we live in, learn about different cultures, go on crazy adventures and feel true joy within yourself. I once attended an event and the guest speaker said that we should view our self-doubt and imposter syndrome thoughts as self-protection. She said that whenever we're about to step outside of our comfort zones, self-doubt will start to creep in, but this is just our minds' way of protecting us because we're not familiar with what we're about to do. I love this way of viewing the situation and I think of this whenever I feel doubt arising.

If anything, travel strengthens your belief that you *are* good enough for anything you want to achieve. Without travel, I probably wouldn't have grown as mentally strong as I am, I wouldn't have had the courage to move abroad and I definitely wouldn't have been writing this book. Travel brings you amazing opportunities, it broadens your perspective and it pushes you to grow and become a better human. Trust yourself enough to know that you can handle whatever life throws at you, you have the power to change how you think.

Go solo! If you have even the slightest urge to travel, don't worry about what other people might say, don't wait around for your friend to go with you, don't suppress your dreams for other people.

I know it's hard to take the leap. Seriously, I know. But it's the same with anything in life—exercising is hard, but so is having health conditions later on in life. Getting through three to four years of university or waking up extra early to work on your new business is hard, but so is being broke. You need to choose which of the two difficult choices you prefer. Growth is painful and change is painful, but is it as painful as being stuck where you are if that's not where you truly want to be?

There is a reason you feel called to travel. The **Adventurer's Mindset** is all about having a sense of curiosity wherever you are in the world. Be willing to learn new things. Your self-awareness will increase and you'll take risks to step into the unknown. When I hear others talk about their experiences while travelling, I can hear the joy in their voices; travel radiates joy and happiness around the world.

By taking the first step and setting off on your travels, you have already adopted a number of these characteristics. When I travelled for the first time, I didn't have much self-awareness and I wasn't too bothered about learning anything new. I didn't notice much of a change within myself during my trip. It was only when I came back home that everything started to change. I noticed I viewed everything differently.

I was immensely grateful for my life every single day.

I started to understand myself a little better and started saying yes to new opportunities. When I saw the difference that travel had made to my life, I knew I needed to go and do it all over again. I had caught the 'travel bug'.

If you still find yourself experiencing limiting beliefs, write them down. Then ask yourself, are these beliefs true? How can I change these beliefs? What is driving my desire to travel solo? Who do I want to *be*? Why do I *really* want this? Limiting beliefs and fears are demons that hold us back from doing the things we want to; they hold us back from achieving our highest potential. You need to get clarity on your vision.

A woman I met while travelling said something which has stuck with me, "You find out more about yourself, what it is you love to do and what it is you're good at by doing more than you do by thinking."

A lot of people will think about doing something or say they want to do something, but they never take the action to go through with it. I'm sure we've all done this in some areas of our lives, but don't let travel be one of those areas. Explore the world, see what it has to offer you and don't let anything hold you back—do the work to remove the blocks and limiting beliefs that are preventing you from living it up.

> *"It is confidence in our bodies, minds and spirits that allows us to keep looking for new adventures, new directions to grow in, and new lessons to learn—which is what life is all about."*
>
> Oprah Winfrey—American talk show host

Are you staying where you are, because you're happy with where your life is at right now? Or are you staying where you are, because you're afraid of trying something new?

@elizacroft_

I SOUND LIKE YOUR PARENTS—
Is Solo Travel Safe For Women?

SAFETY

The main reason many women don't travel solo, is their fear of it not being safe. According to a study made by *Female Solo Travellers Club*, safety worries decrease from 75% to 52% for females who have completed more than 10 solo trips.

In all honesty, there is not one country I've been to so far where I haven't felt safe travelling alone, because you hardly ever end up being *alone*. I have felt uncomfortable, but never unsafe.

There are common safety precautions you should know about before planning to travel alone. Some of these tips may sound like common sense, or something your parents would tell you, but I'll remind you of them anyway.

The first and most important safety tip: ◼ **never tell a stranger that you're travelling alone**. Make something up, tell them you're here with a group of friends who are coming to meet you soon, show them your fake wedding ring, or tell them that you're here with your body-builder boyfriend. Do not tell anyone you're alone.

My next safety tip is to ▣ **always have mobile data on your phone**. If you ever get lost you can use Google Maps to find your way home. Without data, you might find yourself walking in the wrong direction or hopping from café to cafe just to connect to Wi-Fi, which can be quite time-consuming. You should also download an app called 'maps.me', which enables you to use maps without having an internet connection. Just make sure you download the map of the country while you have an internet connection before attempting to use it when you're lost and without a signal. You can get mobile data by buying a SIM card from whichever country you're in. They are available in airports and there are also mobile phone shops in most places. They are usually cheap and will just need a top-up every month.

▣ **Always act like you know where you're going, even when you don't**. It's clear you're not familiar with the area when you're looking at your phone. If you need to use Google Maps, put your earphones in to listen to the directions.

> *HAVING NO DATA ON MY PHONE WAS A BIG MISTAKE I MADE ON my first solo trip. I thought that the only way to avoid an extortionate phone bill was to keep my phone on aeroplane mode and café hop to find Wi-Fi. I'll never know why I didn't realise that it was so easy to get a SIM card. I consider myself to be an averagely smart person, but I can't deny that I'd probably score a four on the scale-of-one-to-common-sense.*
>
> *I arrived in Vietnam not knowing anyone. I had no idea where to go and of course, I had no mobile phone data. I eventually arrived at a hostel in Hanoi after the transfer driver dropped me off in the wrong area. After an eleven-hour flight and a thirty-minute walk with my 20kg backpack (pack light, girls), I felt like I was about to pass out in the humid Vietnamese heat.*

I asked the receptionist for recommendations on where to visit. She passed me a big paper map and told me to turn right to find Hoan Kiem Lake. I followed her instructions and after I'd been walking for what seemed like a while, I took out my paper map as if I were living in the 1960s and I noticed that I was quite far away from the lake. I saw a lovely Vietnamese woman sitting on the steps outside her shop, so I kindly asked for directions but she waved her arms at me and shooed me away like a stray animal. Now I realise that she probably didn't speak English and didn't think she'd be much help to me. Or perhaps she was just having a bad day. Either way, at the time I took offence to her arm waving and felt my eyes starting to tear up (it had been a long day and this tipped me over the edge).

Still extremely lost in an unfamiliar country, I made a second attempt at asking for help from another local lady. The woman pointed me back in the direction I had come from and told me to turn right. As I turned the corner, I bumped into a friend whom I'd met in Bali a few weeks earlier. I couldn't believe it. I knew he was going to Vietnam but I had no idea what area he would be staying in; it turned out we were staying in the same hostel as well! I felt like my life had just been saved, no longer a lost little girl. He had recently moved to Vietnam and he was meeting some friends that night who invited me along to party and eat Vietnamese food. As soon as I was meeting other people, my confidence in solo travelling was back and I was able to complete the rest of the trip alone (well done me).

So, here are a few lessons I learned from this experience:
- ◈ Buy a SIM card to get mobile data
- ◈ Download maps.me app
- ◈ Meet people at the hostel first before attempting to explore the area alone

- ◈ Listen to directions carefully
- ◈ Learn how to read a paper map
- ◈ Not everyone speaks English (and it's ignorant to assume they do)
- ◈ Don't ring your mum telling her you got lost, unless you want her to have a breakdown
- ◈ The universe has your back

Back to the parental safety tips—carrying a ▣ **portable charger** is helpful if you're on long day trips with no access to electricity. This increases your safety if your phone runs out of charge. I'd also recommend purchasing a multi-country adaptor plug, instead of arriving in a country and not being able to charge your phone. I recently did that.

▣ **Don't walk or drive anywhere when it's dark**. Especially when alone, walking around an unfamiliar place in the dark can put you in vulnerable situations. Most places have friendly locals and low crime rates but you can never be too cautious at night. The same goes for driving, especially in Asia if you drive a moped. All the crazy drivers come out at night, as well as the people looking to steal your purse or phone.

There may be situations where you can't avoid walking alone in the dark. If you're out at night, stick to busy main roads.

This brings me to the next tip: ▣ **Stick to crowds**, a well-known safety precaution but something we might turn a blind eye to when we're abroad. You might be tempted to take the shortcut down the dark alley, but it's much safer to stick to lively parts of a city. If you can't avoid quiet areas, use a trusted taxi company. It's safer than walking.

In some countries, the crime rate increased during the pandemic; a small number of the friendly locals are now more desperate to find money to feed their families. Unfortunately, this has resulted in a higher number of robberies. It's very unlikely to happen, but cannot be ruled out. I haven't personally had anything stolen from me while travelling, but I have friends that have. Always keep your bag at the front or around your body, 'bum bags' are very useful to have.

◘ **Stick to trusted taxi companies.** You can research the best taxi company to use in each country. There are lots of taxi drivers on the streets that will try to get you to go with them. While they might genuinely just be trying to get business, there will be the odd ones that might not be legit and you have to be careful. Well-known online taxi companies are probably the best to go for. In Europe or America, Uber is a good option. In Asia, you might use Grab, Lyft, Gojek or JoyRide.

ALTHOUGH ONLINE COMPANIES ARE USUALLY SAFER TO GO WITH, I had a bad experience in Bali which I'd heard of happening quite often.

I ordered a moped taxi via an online app and my driver got pulled over while we were driving. A group of local men told me to get off the moped and go with them instead.

"Online taxis aren't allowed here," they said.

I knew not to go with them. I asked my driver to carry on driving and I even offered the men money to allow me to go with the online taxi company. They refused the money, which quickly made me realise that their intentions may not just have been getting an extra taxi fare. I got off the moped and walked back home. Although I was shaken up, I was grateful that they hadn't tried to physically force me to go with them. I was shocked that this happened to a few people, as Indonesians are some of the friendliest people I'd ever met. I always felt safe living in Bali, but unfortunately, there's a small group that aren't as friendly and they are known as the 'online taxi mafia'.

▣ **Tell people where you are in case anything happens.** This could be a friend or someone at your accommodation. When you're in your own country, you most likely tell people where you are, or someone will know that you're at work at certain times or on a night out at the weekend; it shouldn't be any different when you travel to a different country. It's an extremely important but simple safety precaution to take.

▣ **Create boundaries and trust your intuition**, especially with men. I've gone back and forth deciding whether to include this topic in the book, as I thought the first thing people would say was, "But it's not *all* men."

Women know it's not *all* men, but it happens to almost *all* women.

I spoke to a few travellers about this subject, both men and women, and they all agreed it's a subject that needs to be explored.

You need to learn how to handle unwanted attention from men.

It's extremely common for men to approach women who are alone and the only way a woman can conquer this is by creating boundaries. It's sad and frightening that this happens frequently, but it's reality. This probably won't ever completely stop happening, so although women shouldn't have to deal with it, our reality is that we have to learn how to address it, we need to be informed and assertive.

If a man approaches you when you're alone and this is unwanted attention, you need to get comfortable with saying, "Please leave me alone."

It's the only way men seem to get the message. If you do not want them around, you should not engage in conversation, otherwise they interpret this as though you want to be in their company. I once asked a guy where the bathroom was at a beach party and he followed me around for the rest of the night. So if anyone is looking for a chat-up line, there you go. You should not put yourself alone with a man you're not interested in, because unless you directly tell them, they think you are.

In the past, I've responded to men in such a way that I don't come across as rude, but it turned out that this wasn't enough for them to leave me alone. Since then, I've created boundaries. If any man gives me unwanted attention when I'm alone, I will give off every sign that I'm not interested, to the point where I'll literally tell him. It's the same with social media; I used to respond to all messages because I'd hate for anyone to think I was rude. But in most cases, it's shown me that men seem to think you're interested if you reply.

I COULD MAKE A LONG LIST OF UNCOMFORTABLE SITUATIONS I'VE been in with men while travelling. I was once walking down a street alone and a man pulled over on his motorbike beside me. I walked away and he continued to drive next to me until I told him to leave me alone.

Another time, I was eating alone in a buffet restaurant. I could feel a man staring right at me the entire time I was there. I moved to a table where he couldn't see me. He finished his food and moved to the table next to mine, staring right at me while I was eating.

When a friend of mine was walking to the gym one day, a man on the street flashed her.

In a hostel I stayed in, a man about fifteen years older than me followed me to the kitchen every time he heard me come out of my room. He would sit right in front of me when I was trying to eat breakfast. He would stand right behind me when I was filling up my water bottle and he even knocked on my door at 10.30pm. I would never answer the door to anyone at that time. I knew it couldn't possibly be the accommodation staff as they would send me a message beforehand. I waited until I heard him walk away, back into his room next door. It got to a point where I didn't want to leave my room because I knew he'd be there, waiting. Eventually, he left, but if this had gone on for much longer, I don't think I'd have stayed.

My friend Sarah and I, who I met while solo travelling, once asked a guy to take our photo on a wooden swing in the sea. He seemed like a nice guy, quite a bit older than us, and he was with a group of friends all queuing up to get their photo taken too. We noticed him take the photo of us on his own phone, which was an instant red flag. He said his camera quality was better. He got Sarah's Instagram so he 'could send the photos' (which decreases the quality anyway). When we were out drinking later that night, he turned up to the bar we were at not long after. Coincidence or stalker?

Sarah said hello to be polite and the guy then wouldn't leave her alone. We went downstairs to the bathroom, but when we came out, he was standing outside the Ladies. We told our male friend Glenn, and he tried distracting the guy while we ran out of the bar as fast as we could. The guy followed. We ran past our hotel. We jumped into the nearest place which was a kitchen of a closed restaurant. We hid behind the ovens and watched him walking past, still with Glenn. We left it a few minutes and then ran back to our hotel, while leaving Glenn alone with him (there's a reason we're friends with him, he's one of the good guys and the hero of our night). If you're wondering, Glenn did eventually get back to our hotel safe and sound. He was shocked at what us girls have to put up with.

These situations have all been extremely uncomfortable. It's difficult for us girls not to perceive all men as potential threats as this abuse is something we deal with often. We have to keep our boundaries high, because men behaving like that is extremely common and something that women have experienced for a long time. As much as we don't want to face telling men that these things happen, because we think they'll presume we're talking about all men, including themselves, we need to make them aware that it's not appropriate to cross our boundaries or put us in uncomfortable situations.

Now I bet some of you are thinking, 'Why would I want to travel alone when I might encounter situations like that?'

Just remember that this can happen wherever you are in the world, even in your home town. It can happen with guys you know, guys who you think are your friends or guys you think you can trust. The guys you know can try to take advantage of you when you're drunk, or when they're drunk themselves, even when you clearly tell them, "No" or "Leave me alone". The guys that you know can sometimes be the ones who won't listen. When it happens with people we know well, it forces us to put our guard up even more than it already was, because our minds subconsciously start to think that if we can't trust the guys who we thought were our friends or even partners, who can we trust?

Some guys may act this way out of shyness. Maybe they don't know how to approach a female. Others may be downright annoying. Others may hurt you. If you're unsure, it's not worth taking the risk.

Be open to new relationships and new connections with people who you want to be around, but keep your boundaries set in place for those people you'd prefer to avoid.

I met some amazing guys while travelling and they've outweighed the number of inappropriate guys I've met. In the Philippines, I travelled with two guys who became good, genuine friends and it was a breath of fresh air having them around. I could finally let my guard down and relax because I wouldn't have people shouting over to me on the streets or trying to talk to me all night in the clubs.

If any guys are reading this book, we know the majority of you are amazing people, it's just important for you to be aware that these things happen when females are alone.

◘ **Don't believe everything you hear**. When going to a new country, it's difficult to distinguish between those locals and travellers that are genuine and those who are trying to scam you. When I first arrived in Indonesia, I fell for a scam. I've been debating whether I should write about it, because it was a horrible experience and I wouldn't want it to put anyone off from going. I've decided to add it here just to raise awareness that these things can happen and not to fall victim to them.

◘ **Scams.** I travelled from Croatia – London – Zurich – Bangkok, smoother than ever.

HOWEVER, AT MY LAST DESTINATION, I ARRIVED AT IMMIGRATION and they asked me 101 questions. They made me believe that I didn't arrive on the correct visa, they escorted me and my sister to an immigration office and held us there for four hours. As you can imagine, we were terrified of getting deported. We had been travelling for two and a half days and using the airport floor as our bed. They took our phones from us. They used their power to look through all of our WhatsApp messages and photos from our camera roll (definitely not allowed, but because we were so terrified, we did as they said).

At this point, we truly believed we were on the wrong visa and thought that we were at fault. After hours of being sat around a conference table with the officers offering us cigarettes, we were told that immigration was negotiating whether to let us into the country or not. Of course, this negotiation included scamming us out of a large amount of money. With me being desperate to get into the country to live there long-term, and the officers managing to convince me I was on the wrong visa, I was more than happy to pay this.

As soon as we paid, they let us go. They had taken advantage of two young girls and we shamefully fell for it. You live and you learn, I guess. I felt a responsibility as I was the older sister who should have been taking care of my 18-year-old sister. I tried to act like everything was fine, but in reality, I was waking up anxious for the next three nights thinking that the police were going to come knocking on my door to tell us we'd be deported.

Scams are everywhere and you have to be careful. Here's me, trying to convince you to go travelling while telling you horror stories. They don't happen often (I was just unlucky) and you shouldn't let this story hold you back.

However, I think that raising awareness is key to stopping situations like this from repeating themselves. Not everything is a scam and there are more genuine people than not. If something seems off, it might well be. Use your instinct, it will be your best friend while travelling.

Overall, as a female solo traveller I have never once felt unsafe or at risk, with the exception of the airport horror story and encountering a few creepy guys. Safety should be kept in mind with all decisions you make while travelling. Especially when travelling solo, which forces you to be aware of your surroundings and personal safety, whereas in a group it may be natural to expose your vulnerability by letting your guard down. As long as you take the necessary precautions you will more than likely be well and safe.

The people who tell you that travelling isn't safe are the people who have never travelled. They're the people who have watched the travel horror stories that the media has chosen to show to you. The world has beautiful places, beautiful people and so much joy; but the media will never show this side of travelling. That's why people who have never travelled have a misconception about what it's really like. So next time someone places doubts in your head, ask yourself, has this person ever travelled? You should never take advice from someone who has never done the thing that you're wanting to do.

When I first mentioned to some friends about wanting to travel to the Philippines alone, a number of them told me not to go there because 'it's not safe', and 'why would you want to go there when you can stay in Bali?' Bearing in mind these people had never been to the Philippines before, I took my own advice and didn't listen to anyone who hadn't done what I wanted to do. Instead, I listened to the people who *had* visited the Philippines and were telling me it was one of the best places they'd ever been to. Now I've been, I can confirm it's a stunning place with friendly people and I'm so glad I didn't listen to those that were trying to talk me out of it.

As I always do when I solo travel, I easily met friends. I made friends the second I walked into my hostel room and ended up doing day trips with the girls I met there. I had other people message me on social media to say they were there too. It was one of the best experiences I've ever had. The Philippines had been at the top of my bucket list for years, so when I decided I wanted a change from Bali, it made sense to finally tick it off the list.

Safety worries decrease from 75% to 52% for females who have completed more than 10 solo trips.

Female Solo Travellers Club

HEALTH

When it comes to your health, it's important to be prepared before setting off on your travels. Ensure you stock up on medications or daily needed health products such as contact lenses and birth control pills. You should also check with your GP if there are any vaccines you may need before visiting certain countries. You may be able to get specific travel vaccines from your GP, but for others, you may need to pay for them at a travel clinic. To be prepared, you should give yourself at least two months before your departure date to start looking into what vaccines you may need, as it's recommended to take some vaccines a certain number of weeks before you arrive in the destination country. However, if you decide to travel somewhere last minute like I normally do, don't worry, you'll still be able to get your vaccines from somewhere and it's still ok to get them late. Having any sort of vaccine is your personal choice and you should always check with your GP first.

Even if you don't usually get travel sick like myself, I'd advise always taking travel sickness tablets with you. I find that when I'm travelling every few days on different types of transport, I start to feel travel sick. Other travellers have also told me they felt the same.

◙ **Don't forget your travel insurance.** You need to do a little more research into travel insurance than you would for a usual short holiday. There are plenty of insurance companies out there to choose from but if you're travelling long-term, make sure you choose a company that covers the entire period, as most companies only cover short trips. The long-term travel insurance company I use is 'Safety Wing'. At the time of writing, they also include COVID-19 coverage and you can pay monthly, which is convenient if you don't know how long you'll be travelling. I know quite a few travellers who use 'World Nomads' travel insurance; have a shop around and decide which one suits you best.

◙ **Drink a lot more water than usual**. When you're busy enjoying your daily adventures, it's easy to forget to keep hydrated. If you forget, you'll know about it by the end of the day—heat exhaustion will hit you!

◙ **Mosquito spray** will become your perfume when travelling. Mosquitoes are everywhere in hot countries, so make sure you always carry mosquito cream or spray wherever you go if you don't want to be itching from huge red bites all over your body every day.

So now I've drilled some health and safety rules into your head, which are probably the same things your parents have told you fifty million times, let's move on to something else.

WELLBEING

We sometimes get caught up in the thrill of travelling and we forget to take time for ourselves to relax and recharge. Days of doing nothing are allowed. Listen to your body and if you feel like it needs rest, then take a day out from the parties and adventures. Yesterday was one of those days for me, I knew I needed to feel calmness and peace, so I drove myself to the beach in the early hours of the morning when no one else was around, I found a peaceful spot, meditated to the sound of the waves, wrote in my journal and read my book.

From taking that time for myself in the morning, the rest of the day followed precisely. Yesterday was the day of peace and calmness that my body and mind needed. Solo travel is about meeting new people, but it's also about becoming comfortable with being alone.

It's completely normal to get homesick when you're away from home for a long period, especially on occasions like Christmas and birthdays. I find that I start to miss the little things from home. I miss taking my dogs on walks, I miss the big family get-togethers and I miss sitting around the dinner table every Sunday eating a Sunday roast while my nana has us all in tears of laughter.

WHEN I FIRST MOVED TO INDONESIA, I MET A FRIEND THAT HAD already lived there for two years. Although he made me super excited for my upcoming life-changing experience, he also gave me some home truths for what I was about to face. He told me that six months into him being away from home, he experienced serious homesickness. He was really close to booking a flight home because he missed his family and the comforts that came with being in a familiar environment. Two years later he was still in Indonesia, telling me about this time because he knew I was about to experience the same thing.

Four months into being away from home, I was in tears most nights, wondering how I was going to make this life work for me. I missed my friends and family. I was worrying about how I'd keep money coming in. Contact had started to drift from friends back home and all my past relationship traumas I didn't know I had suddenly showed up out of nowhere. What was this horrendous feeling I was experiencing?

Homesickness. The only type of homesickness I'd experienced before was while at a friend's house for a sleepover in primary school. But this was something different. Something I'd never felt before. It was the realisation that I was so far from home, I'd been away for longer than I ever had before and I had no plan to go back anytime soon.

I remembered what my friend said, I acknowledged this feeling and I let the emotions come through. After a few weeks, the feeling disappeared. I want to reiterate the story my friend told me, as many of you will experience the same thing, just as I did.

This feeling of aching and longing could be for the things you take comfort in at home, like the food you're used to eating. It could be for being in the home environment itself or for the people you love. I find that it helps to bring familiar items from home or photos of loved ones. Keep in touch with friends and family back home. Video-call them often so it feels like they're just around the corner.

Time zones can be difficult when wanting to keep in touch with family and friends. I've found the thing that works best for me is to arrange specific days and times to call friends. At first, this feels strange as you wouldn't usually have to add your friends to your diary, but it's harder to call them when you're on opposite sides of the world. For family or friends that you speak to every day, figure out a time that works best for all of you. For example, my mum will call me every day as soon as she wakes up because this time is also good for me.

You should prepare yourself to drift away from certain people back home. It's sad, but it's reality. They may not mean anything by it, everyone has their own lives going on, but sometimes when you're travelling alone you appreciate the home comfort that comes from a FaceTime call with a friend.

Some may think you don't need support, comfort, love or just to hear a friendly voice while you're solo travelling because of course, every day you're 'living your best life'.

Feelings and emotions don't disappear when you travel, you take them along with you and you go through the motions. Understand that it's normal to have little, if any, contact with some friends and family. This doesn't mean you're unloved or lonely, which is easy to believe when you notice this starting to happen. There's a lot you can't control, so just control what you can.

That being said, you need to also remember that your friends and family are missing you too. You have a responsibility to keep in touch with them and update them on your adventures. They could also be experiencing loneliness from you not being around, so you need to check in with them. You will know the right time to take a step back if you feel your effort isn't being reciprocated.

Try to keep busy so you don't overthink too much, but remember, you're allowed days off and you should allow yourself time to think about what's on your mind at certain points in the week. Although overthinking can increase homesickness, ◼ **if you do feel homesick then make sure you acknowledge it,** and know that no matter how intense your homesickness is at the moment, this feeling will not last forever. It helps to talk to other people about it and they may be able to give you some advice if they've experienced it too.

When travelling, it's easy to fall out of routine, so trying to ◼ **implement a small daily routine**, whether this is morning or night, might help decrease the feeling of there being too many changes. My morning routine consists of meditating, journaling, reading and body movement, whether this is going to the gym or just doing some stretches in my bedroom. My routine takes me around one hour to complete, so I get up one hour earlier than I need to each day to fit it in. It took me a while to build this routine, but I did it by habit stacking (starting with one thing, then when that becomes a habit, add the next). This routine won't work for everyone, but it works for me.

To create your own self-care rituals, you may need to experiment with different practices to find out what makes you feel your best. It could be going for a walk in the morning or just sitting by yourself drinking a morning coffee. It shouldn't have to be a chore, just do whatever it is that makes you feel good.

Another thing that helps me with homesickness is listening to songs that remind me of home; my parents used to play Elton John in the kitchen, so I'll shamefully admit I've listened to his songs on repeat while travelling. I haven't yet been homesick enough to start listening to Coldplay though, that's a bad music choice from my mum.

If homesickness is one of your biggest worries, I would suggest travelling to a country not too far from home first. If you decide you don't like travelling, home is only a short flight away. I feel an increase in homesickness when I first arrive in a new country and you may experience this too, especially if it's your first time travelling. It's completely normal to feel like this when you're in an unfamiliar place and you haven't met many other people there yet.

The first few days of being in Thailand, I felt extremely homesick and overwhelmed; I wasn't sure why, as I'd travelled alone so much before, but this felt different. I had to sit and reflect and I realised that it was because I hadn't met new people as soon as I arrived like I usually do in other countries. I had come to Thailand intending to do no travelling or meeting up with people every day. I'd come to find a place to live and get my head down to finish this book and work. Although it was my choice not to be meeting up with new people and I knew I usually found it quite easy, I still experienced feelings of loneliness and being homesick. Sometimes no matter how experienced you are with solo travelling, homesickness is a feeling that may creep up in different situations or at different periods during your travels.

As well as the holistic side to keeping healthy, diet and exercise are also important when travelling long-term. I must put a disclaimer here to say that I'm in no way an expert on this subject. I can already see my friends who are fitness coaches shaking their heads thinking 'what is she talking about?' But I'll talk about this from my point of view and my experience of diet and exercise while travelling.

It's easy to forget that not every day is a Saturday when you're travelling, and although you might be able to party every other night for the first month or so, after a while it will get too much and you might find that you need to limit the party days. There are so many amazing, once-in-a-lifetime activities to do in the daytime, so you don't want to waste too many days in bed feeling sorry for yourself. However, if partying is what you're going there to do, then go for it, the world has some unreal nightlife scenes!

There are gyms and sports facilities in most places. I have even seen free gyms on beaches, where the weights are made out of stone or wood. If you can make it to the gym or attend an exercise class a few times a week, then that's great. If not, it's handy to bring small workout accessories with you, like a resistance band or skipping rope. These are small enough to fit in your bag and you can still have a good, impactful work-out by using them a few times a week. And if you don't fancy packing those, just try doing some bodyweight exercises in your room or outside—there are lots of workouts to choose from on YouTube.

As well as being a great way to meet new people, attending new exercise classes is also a fun way to keep healthy while travelling. It's nice to find different ways to move your body and experience activities that you don't often find in your home country. You will also find yourself spending more time outdoors than you would at home, which is extremely good for your health.

Although you're 'on your holidays', and you should be able to eat more of what you want and enjoy it without feeling guilty, if you're travelling long-term, you might find that your change in diet will decrease your energy after a while. Even if you're eating out most of the time, you should try to keep a balanced diet and not just eat pancakes every day for breakfast (no matter how tempting this might seem, and I can't deny that I didn't do this myself).

You will most likely know your own body and what kind of diet best suits you. Not everyone needs the same amount of exercise or the same diet to keep healthy while travelling. This mainly depends on which body type you are (ectomorph, mesomorph or endomorph). It's useful to know which body type you are so that you can have a better understanding of what food you should be prioritising in your diet and how much exercise to fit in.

People often think that their diet and exercise will fly out of the window once they start travelling. This isn't always the case. If you're on a skiing trip or a hiking holiday, then you're already incorporating your daily exercise. If you're travelling to a hotter country where you won't be engaging in exercise every day, you might just need to plan your workouts a little more than if you were going on an active trip. You could go on a run around the area you're staying, before it gets too hot, if you're awake early enough; unless you're staying in certain areas of Bali, where the pavements have huge gaping holes that you can quite easily fall into, or people who routinely ride their mopeds on the pavements rather than the road. In this case, I'd avoid running altogether or find a treadmill.

When travelling long-term, you also need to ensure you're getting high-quality sleep.

Cue: Eyes rolled by people who think sleep is for the weak.

It's fun to have late nights every once in a while (or more often when you're travelling), but take notice when you start to feel burned out, and make sure you catch up on sleep. After a while, it gets difficult when you have a full day of adventure ahead of you and you've only slept for six hours in the last four days. If you're in a hot country, take advantage of sunbathing and have a nap while you catch a tan, or use the travel time on ferries, sleeper trains or long car journeys to catch up on your sleep.

As well as saving you money in particular countries, cooking yourself can also help keep your diet balanced. You will know exactly what you're putting into your body, which makes it easier for you to see whether you're sticking to a balanced diet. Of course, this is only possible if you stay in an apartment or villa, as you will need a kitchen and fridge. If you want to concentrate on your diet, it's a good idea to research the food before you check out the views of other travellers. People might suggest getting an apartment so that you can cook at home, and in some countries, you can get healthy and cheap meals delivered every day.

When your days are jam-packed with activities, it's easy to skip meals, unless you're like me, then it's almost impossible to forget to eat. I get hungry every two hours. Skipping meals can throw you off track with your diet and decrease your energy. It's good to plan your meal times around your activities so that you know you won't be skipping any meals and snacking on crisps instead. If you want the crisps though, go ahead and eat them without feeling guilty; I have no authority to tell someone not to snack when I'm the queen of snacking myself.

Let me be realistic, you will not stick to healthy eating and exercising every single day while you're travelling. If you can do this, can you share the secret with me? There will be long days where you'll be travelling for most of the day, there will be days where you'll be hungover in bed questioning your life decisions and there will be days where you just really cannot be bothered and would much rather sunbathe on the beach all day. You travel to enjoy life, don't put too much pressure on yourself to stick to all these healthy habits. You could even forget everything I've mentioned in this chapter if you wanted to, but just try to avoid getting sick as much as possible, the bugs you catch abroad are not pleasant.

Overall, travelling will have huge benefits on your wellbeing. Here are some of the benefits, travel can offer:

- ◈ Conquers fears
- ◈ Gain knowledge & understanding of the world
- ◈ Pushes you out of your comfort zone
- ◈ Enhances your creativity
- ◈ Exposes you to new opportunities
- ◈ Improves social and communication skills
- ◈ Increases your self-awareness
- ◈ Improves your mental, physical and emotional health
- ◈ Helps you recharge and relieve stress
- ◈ You receive real-life education

*You travel to enjoy life.
Don't put too much
pressure on yourself.*

@elizacroft_

FINDING THE (NOT SO)
PERFECT ACCOMMODATION

The prism through which you make decisions can change by using the Adventurer's Mindset. When it comes to finding the right accommodation, it can be tricky if you're looking for everything to be perfect. One thing travel teaches you is to not care too much about where you're staying. You won't be spending much time in your room, so you might not want to be staying somewhere really expensive, unless money isn't an issue for you. but most first-time travellers just want cheap and cheerful. Using the Adventurer's mindset, you can push the idea of choosing accommodation only for comfort to the side, and instead think about meeting new people to travel with or budgeting so that you can prolong your travels.

Booking.com, Airbnb, Agoda, Hostel World, and Hotels.com are all good sites to find cheap accommodation tailor-made for travellers. Always make sure they offer the correct protection, such as ABTA. If you can find contact details for the accommodation, try contacting them directly and they might offer you a cheaper rate, or do something to make your stay more pleasant like give you free breakfast or a lovely welcome note. If you're booking on Airbnb, you can click on the 'contact host' option which will put you directly in touch with the host and they'll then usually give you a cheaper rate than what the online booking site offers. I've found that sticking to the same booking site can save you money too—a lot of booking sites offer rewards and discounts to loyal customers.

Sharing accommodation can work out a lot cheaper overall. If you find a friend who wants to travel to the same places as you, sharing a room will save you some money. You can also choose room-sharing options in hostels which works out cheaper. If you're wanting to stay in a private room by yourself, you could contact the accommodation directly to see if they'll give you a discount for single occupancy so that you can save some money. You should check whether any major events are taking place in the area during the time you intend to stay, as this may increase the price of accommodation and flights.

Here are some top tips for staying in hostels:

- ◈ Don't turn the main light on early in the morning or late at night unless you want to have some annoyed roommates. Use your phone torch or bedside lamp instead.
- ◈ If you're leaving early hours of the morning, make sure you pack your bags the night before, so that you're not thudding around at 5am, waking everyone up.

    I stayed in a co-working hostel in the Philippines—a completely different vibe from the usual party hostels I've stayed in; people were up at 4.30am to start work instead of only just getting in from a night out at that time. If you stay in a hostel you might need to accept that other people's sleeping habits aren't the same as your own and you will get woken up at unusual times, even if you're a deep sleeper like me.
- ◈ Never hold up the bathroom. You might have all the time in the world to get ready, but your roommate could be in a rush to go out while you're dancing around in the shower.

◈ One tip that might seem like common sense to some, but clearly wasn't to me, is to always check which bed is yours.

IN VIETNAM, I STAYED IN MY FIRST EVER HOSTEL, I WALKED INTO my room and chose a random bed that had the curtain open. I then wondered why my locker key wasn't working for that specific bed number, only to come back a few hours later, climb up onto my bed and find I was sitting there with someone else's bags and teddy bear. Only then did I realise that I was in the wrong bed and the other person had dumped my belongings on the floor.

Another tip I've learnt along the way is to never book the accommodation for the full duration you plan to stay (unless it's peak season). There's been many times where I've booked somewhere for a week and then either not liked it or there was some sort of issue with the place. I now always book the place for one or two nights and then extend if I'm happy there. During a Christmas period, me and the friends I met in Bali booked a villa. When we arrived on Christmas Eve, it didn't look anything like the pictures online and there was mould everywhere, so we had to go off and search for another one. It's not what you want on Christmas Eve, but it worked out well as the next villa we found was amazing and we had the best time celebrating our first Christmas away from home.

You should keep the address of your hotel somewhere handy, but not somewhere where you'll need Wi-Fi to access it.

You should never tell anyone where you're staying. If they ask, be vague, even with taxis. I usually wait until they've driven off so they don't watch me walk into the exact place I'm staying at.

If you're not fussy, finding accommodation is usually quite simple, so you don't always need to book in advance. However, if you're planning to travel in peak season, I would recommend having a look in advance. If you do book accommodation before you travel, I'd recommend ◼ **booking places that offer free cancellation,** in case any issues prop up beforehand. There have been several times where I've booked accommodation on the day I plan to arrive, some even a few hours before.

That's the beauty of travelling, you have the freedom and flexibility to choose wherever you want to be whenever you want to be there.

That said, I recently booked a bed in a female hostel dormitory a few hours before I arrived. The hostel was unaware of my booking and there was no bed available in the female room, only in the mixed gender room. Now there's nothing wrong with men (or *most* men should I say), but I generally feel safer staying in a female-only room. The only time I've made an exception with staying in a mixed dormitory room is when I met a group of friends while travelling, both male and female, and we decided to travel together to the next place and stay in the same hostel room.

Now I'm not sure how well this paragraph will age as travel seems to be getting back to normal, but in this modern-day world, we also need to take quarantine accommodation into account. Ensure you check the travel restrictions for each country you visit to see if you need to quarantine on arrival. For the countries where you do need to complete a period of quarantine, there will be a list of specific quarantine hotels to choose from. You should contact these hotels directly to make them aware that your stay is for quarantine purposes. If you book on a normal booking site, the hotel will not be aware you're completing quarantine and therefore they won't make arrangements for food, PCR tests and your completed quarantine certification to be provided to you. I hope that one day this paragraph can be discarded from this book, but for now, it's still a step we need to consider.

If you do find yourself having to complete quarantine, please look at the *recent* reviews for your quarantine hotel, from guests who have also completed quarantine there.

THE HOTEL THAT I BOOKED LOOKED LIKE A NICE 4* HOTEL WITH a lot of good reviews. My sister and I arrived at the hotel feeling like nothing more could go wrong after our traumatic immigration experience. We were given a few minutes to go to the shop next door to buy snacks for our eight days of quarantine, as we weren't allowed to get food delivered into the hotel. If I knew what the next eight days had in store for us, I would have bought a full week's worth of shopping.

I had planned to get my sh*t together in quarantine, I planned to exercise most days, get a whole load of work done and organise my whole life. I can confirm that this did not happen as I spent the entire time just trying to survive. Each day, they would either forget to bring us food or we would get given tiny portions of freezing food that wasn't edible. We were those annoying guests who rang reception ten times a day asking where our food was or begging for them to let us order what we wanted from their normal restaurant menu. My favourite meal was probably the breakfast they brought to us most mornings, which was two slices of bread with jam and chocolate sprinkles, (I know, I'd never heard of anything like it before either, but at least the bread stopped us from starving).

When they eventually agreed to us requesting our own food, we were over the moon until they got almost every order wrong.

We tried to order chicken legs and then got a WhatsApp message from the hotel saying, "These?" with a picture of chicken feet that still had the nails on. Could you imagine our faces if they'd brought them up to our room? I've since learned that this meal is common in some Asian countries, but at this point, if we hadn't laughed, we would have cried. We both lost so much weight and I don't mean to be dramatic, but the whole time felt like we were on the TV show 'I'm A Celebrity... Get Me Out Of Here'.

And you *are* a celebrity when you're travelling in your own new world, with all the sense of drama, adventure, revelation, and memorable stories.

You have the freedom and flexibility to choose wherever you want to be, whenever you want to be there.

@elizacroft_

ON THE ROAD

From flights to ferries, trains, overnight sleeper buses and campervan trips, I've tried them all. Today, getting around is easier and more affordable than ever. The more you travel, the more you pick clever, effective ideas for comfortable and good value modes of transportation.

How do you know which to choose?

Ask yourself these questions:

- ◈ Am I travelling internationally or domestically?
- ◈ What is my budget?
- ◈ How much time do I have?
- ◈ Do I want to help the environment?

If you are travelling to the opposite side of the world, catching a flight is the obvious answer. However, if you are travelling between countries that are not that far from each other, you may consider other forms of transport. I like to use the app 'Rome2Rio' to help me decide on the best transport for my journey.

TRAINS/BUSES

Catching the bus or train is easy and cost-effective. If you have the flexibility and timeframe to catch a train rather than a flight, I'd recommend looking into this option. You can even travel overnight, which effectively saves you one night accommodation and a costly flight fee.

There are different classes of trains and buses. The overnight trains are generally more comfortable than the buses, as well as slightly more expensive. One thing you should take into account when booking, is that the lower beds are usually slightly bigger than the upper beds. I really enjoy overnight train journeys. I always get a good night's sleep and enjoy getting some time to myself after busy, social travel days.

It is also far more environmentally friendly than catching a flight. Air travel is one of the largest contributors to climate change.

CAMPERVANS

Ever considered going on a road trip? It might be a little different to the type of travel you have in mind, but hiring a campervan to travel to several different places can be so much fun.

I once travelled around Europe in a campervan; it was a great way to see several countries on one trip.

To travel this way, you will need to pre-book campsites to pitch your van at each destination. You should also check that you have the correct license and insurance for driving this type of vehicle. Travelling this way may take a little more planning, but it's definitely an amazing way to see the world.

FERRIES

Ferries are more environmentally friendly and a cheaper option than air travel, although they may take a little longer. You can book them online if you search for ferries to your destination. There are also many stalls and offices around tourist areas that sell boat tickets.

Ferries are widely available across many countries and boats are one of the most scenic ways to travel.

FLIGHTS

If you know the exact destination and dates of your trip and can plan ahead, you will usually find a cheaper rate if you book your flights in advance. I book my flights very last-minute as I make spontaneous travel plans. Sometimes I'm lucky to catch a last-minute deal, but most of the time it works out much more expensive than if I had booked my tickets earlier.

WHEN I SAY LAST MINUTE, I BOOKED MY FLIGHT TO INDONESIA less than 48 hours before travelling, I think it was closer to 24 hours. I definitely wouldn't recommend this though. I was in Croatia at the time that my visa got accepted and I'd been trying to find flights direct from there for days. This turned out to be impossible, unless I was going to pay a ridiculous price. I was on the phone with my friend on a Saturday night and explained that I couldn't find any flights.

He told me he'd have a look into it and within a few hours I got a call-back, "I've found you a flight...but you have to leave Monday morning."

Let's just say, I'd never been as stressed as I was on the Sunday trying to get everything done in one day; I got a same-day PCR, found somewhere in Croatia to print out forms, packed my bags, booked my flight, accommodation and quarantine hotel, filled in online health applications, checked in for my flight and exchanged money, then I left to catch the ferry at 5 am the next morning. Try to plan your travels a little more in advance than this.

There are certain countries where you need to plan ahead. Unlike most other countries in South East Asia, you cannot travel to the Philippines on a budget if you don't plan in advance, as you need to get a lot of internal flights. I thought the internal flights would be around £30 like they are in many other countries, but because I was only booking them the day before, they were over £100 each.

As well as the expense, trying to book transport last minute is near impossible. Transport in the Philippines needs to be booked a few days in advance, as I came to find out when I tried catching a same-day ferry. I was told I couldn't leave the island for another two days until the next ferry was scheduled.

I usually don't like to book my whole trip in advance. I prefer to meet new people first and see where they're going, but you might need to make exceptions for certain countries if you want to make the trip as cheap as possible. It's important to research each country before you visit.

If I wasn't such a last-minute traveller, I'd probably book my flights four to six weeks before. This will give you enough time to get organised. You should book your flights so you don't arrive at night, in case you have a problem with the accommodation when you get there. You don't want to be stranded with nowhere else open until the morning, especially if you're travelling alone. This is exactly what happened to my auntie on her first solo trip to Prague, which resulted in her wandering the streets, trying to find somewhere to stay.

◼ **One way to find the cheapest flights is by using Skyscanner's 'Search Everywhere' feature.** When you click in the destination box, click the 'Can't decide where?' tab and in the departure date box, click 'whole month' and 'cheapest month'. It will then list several different countries with the cheapest deals in the cheapest months. When you click into each country, it will break it down further into cities and airports. You can also ◼ **sign up for email alerts from airlines** two to three months before your planned travel dates. They will send out offers they have on at the time. If you're more concerned about money over convenience, you could consider flying in or out via a smaller airport, as some will be cheaper than your main destination point.

You might have heard that travel agencies are more expensive to book with, but they can often find you great deals that fit your budget. They may also be able to get you great add-ons like free breakfast or late check-outs. Travel agents take the stress away from planning everything yourself and they're on hand if you have any problems during your trip. Some online sites can be cheaper, so it's best to shop around while also considering the risk of not getting your money back with certain online sites. You should keep a look out for which booking sites and airlines are ◼ **ATOL and ABTA protected.**

I would recommend having a look at credit cards that can save you money on flights. Certain card companies use a ◼ **system that builds you points that you can then use to spend on flights** (and many other things too, but we all want the free flights, right?). I use the AMEX credit card to build up points that I use to buy flight tickets. You can also sign up for frequent flyer programs or travel reward programs for specific hotel chains and airlines.

◼ **You should always have a return or onward flight booked** as airport staff will often ask you for proof of this. Last year, I made this mistake when I arrived in Indonesia. If you remember the story of me being held in an immigration office, this was just another reason they had against me. Sometimes the departure airport will ask you for this before they let you go any further, but I got through four different countries without being asked for it until I arrived at my final destination.

If you don't know you're next destination or haven't decided on a return date, you don't have to book a return flight back to your home country. There are two options you can take. The first is to find cheap flights to any nearby country, book for any random day and then cancel it once you're through the airport. The second option is to use an online website called **Onwardticket.com** where you can book an onward flight and the website will hold it for 48 hours for a small fee. As I'm always flexible with travel and I never want to plan an exact date to fly out, I use the Onwardticket.com option, which always works when asked for proof of return flight at the airports. For us open-dated travellers, it could get quite expensive if we were booking return flights and then cancelling them because our plans have changed, but it's just a protocol that the staff at airports have to follow to show that you plan on leaving their country.

SPEAKING OF MISTAKES MADE AT AIRPORTS, MAKE SURE YOU check that the name on your boarding pass matches the name on your passport exactly. The first time I'd ever travelled alone, I arrived at the airport at the last minute along with my upset parents who came to wave me off. I already felt a little stressed because I'd never been to an airport by myself before. In the past, I had always let someone else deal with the check-in process and finding out which gate our flight was departing from. I got to the check-in and handed over my passport. The woman behind the desk said, "Your name on your boarding pass doesn't match the one on your passport, you need to go and change it."

Who else's name could I have possibly entered when I booked my flights? It turned out that my name was just the wrong way around. It read 'Croft Eliza', instead of 'Eliza Croft'. I was already late and now I had to queue up to get my name flipped around on a boarding pass. After a long wait, I quickly said goodbye to my parents and ran for my flight. I also said goodbye to my plans of sitting down in the airport to eat breakfast before my flight (those who know me, know how I can't go about my day without having breakfast). At the time, I was extremely shy and cared a lot about what others thought of me, so having to run through the airport to make my flight was quite the nightmare for me.

You need to have a whole bag of things that will entertain you if it's a long-haul flight. It's great if it's night-time at your destination because you can try to sleep for most of the flight. But if sleeping on flights is impossible for you, it's best to bring books, a notebook and pen, snacks and headphones. Remember to download some podcasts and music before you set off. If it's a long-haul flight, they will usually have screens so that you can watch a few movies to kill time. They also have

USB sockets to charge your phone and most of the time they will give you a blanket, pillow or eye mask. Food is usually included in the price you pay for the flight. When I saw the flight attendant handing out food, I thought I wasn't going to be included as I didn't add it to my booking, but I got given three meals, which I was very grateful for after missing my breakfast at the airport. However, on short-haul flights, you most likely won't receive any of this.

To survive long flights, you should also walk about the plane a few times to keep active, stay hydrated and bring earplugs, comfortable clothes, your toothbrush and face wipes/cleanser. Another thing I like to do on long-haul flights is planning; I'll use it as a brainstorming session and write down my plans for when I arrive, my goals and anything else that comes to mind—this seems to pass quite a lot of time. You should take advantage of this time to relax; if you're about to encounter a crazy, adventurous travel experience with lots of partying, it might be the last chance you get to relax for a while.

If you're someone who tends to get anxious about flying, I would suggest trying relaxation therapy leading up to and during, your flight. This can include practices like meditation, breathing, visualisation exercises and yoga (it might be slightly difficult to start practising your crow pose down the aisle of the plane, but you can definitely try out yoga leading up to the day of your flight). These exercises should relax your mind in preparation for the flight. Turning on the air vents above your head, leaning your head back and closing your eyes should make you feel less claustrophobic. You should learn the built-in safety measures by listening to and watching the demonstration from the flight attendants. Read the information sheets provided, this is important as it can be a slightly different procedure on each flight. Whenever I feel fearful of anything, I like to remember that being worried about something that hasn't happened is of no benefit to you. This applies to any sort of fear you may have, not just the fear of flying. If your fear of flying is extremely severe, but you really want to travel, you may want to seek out professional help to try out other techniques.

So now you've survived your long-haul flight, you need to battle off your jetlag too. Jetlag is worse if you travel from west to east. Symptoms include headaches, fatigue, difficulty concentrating, mood swings, lack of appetite and gastrointestinal conditions. But for me, I just feel like I could sleep for three days straight. There was a time when I was younger when my ankles used to swell up on the plane. For quite a few years, when I heard people talk about jetlag, I always thought they were saying 'jet leg', and that this happened when your legs swell up on the plane as mine did. I can confirm that I was in shock on the day I found out I was completely wrong about this.

There are a few ways you can attempt to battle jet lag and no, Eliza, it's not putting ice packs on your ankles so the swelling disappears. You should try adapting quickly to your new time zone by trying to sleep, wake up and eat at the time that is normal in your new destination. To make it easier to stay awake, you should keep active, expose yourself to daylight and make sure you drink plenty of water.

Now I'm not sure whether this is obvious, or whether I was just young and dumb at the time (maybe I still am), but not everyone on your connecting flight is going to the same end destination as you. Don't follow them. I was twenty years old when I got my first long-haul flight alone, I didn't know what I was doing in regards to connecting flights.

■ **Does everyone on my first flight go to my end destination? Do I collect my bags at every stop-off or does the airline transfer them? Do I need to check in for each separate flight?**

Most airlines will transfer your luggage for you on connecting flights, but you must make sure they do it beforehand by checking your flight booking confirmation or asking the airport staff. You usually don't need to check in for each connecting flight, you will just make your way through transfers to the next gate to board the plane. Unless your flights were booked separately, then you will need to re-check in.

On my first long-haul flight to Hong Kong, I thought I would be able to follow the other passengers through the airport. It turned out that not everyone on my first flight would be catching the connecting flight to my final destination. An obvious mistake. But for this first-time solo traveller, this caused confusion.

Some airports require you to catch a bus to another part of the airport to collect your luggage. The first time I encountered this, I was with my sister and we followed other people to the bus and then noticed that we forgot to collect our luggage. The only way back was to run back up the escalators that were moving downwards. When we made it back up to the top, it was only then we realised that the bus that we were originally queuing up for was going to take us to collect our luggage.

These events made me realise that travelling alone required me to use my brain. I hadn't noticed how much I'd relied on friends and family to direct me through airports in the past. It may seem easy, but when you've never done it before, or you haven't in a few years, then it might take a little getting used to.

I'M NOT THE ONLY ONE WHO STRUGGLED ON THEIR FIRST LONG-HAUL flight. My sister Harriet took her first long-haul flight alone when she was eighteen. At first, she called me, panicking. When she arrived at the airport, she was told that she needed a PCR test for one of the connecting countries she was passing through, even though she didn't need one to arrive back in the U.K. She managed to get this done at the airport before her flight.

Next, I received a WhatsApp message from her saying that her flight had been delayed and she'd only just arrived in her first connecting country, with twenty minutes to spare before her next flight. When she got off the flight, she rang me almost in tears because she didn't know whether she needed to collect her bag before she got on her next flight, which left in ten minutes. I knew in the back of my mind that the gate would have already closed by now and she would have missed her flight.

We agreed that she would leave her bag in hope that it would be automatically transferred and she ran through the airport to try and catch the flight. Ten minutes later she called me back and told me that her flight actually leaves in an hour. She hadn't realised that the time zone she was in now was an hour behind the time her phone was showing. So she'd stressed, cried, left her bag and ran through the airport, all to realise she had an extra hour to chill out before her flight. It turned out that she did have to collect her bags for this connection after all. The lessons to take from this are to always check whether you need to collect your bag before you arrive at the airport and ensure you have the correct time displayed on your phone to avoid unnecessary stress.

When booking your flights, specifically on sites that give options for many different airlines, ensure you check the layover time between connecting flights. Your connecting flight will not wait for you if your previous flight is delayed.

My friend had a problem with this when he was flying out to Bali. His first flight to Berlin was delayed and he only had one hour before his next flight departed. By the time he arrived, the check-in gate had already closed and he was told he couldn't get on the flight. From this, he had to stay overnight in Berlin (at least this allowed him to see another country) and pay for another PCR test, as his other had expired. I thought he'd have learned his lesson from this the first time, but I recently got a text from him to tell me he'd done the exact same thing again and missed his flight to Cambodia.

◪ **So it's always best to make sure you have a few hours before each connecting flight, in case any problems arise.**

"I see my path, but I don't know where it leads. Not knowing where I'm going is what inspires me to travel it."

Rosalia de Castro—Writer and poet

Travelling alone requires you to use your brain.

@elizacroft_

TURNING STRANGERS
INTO LIFELONG FRIENDS

Isn't it lonely and dangerous to travel alone?

Even if you consider yourself a quiet person who finds it uncomfortable starting conversations with strangers, I promise you will l make friends when travelling solo. I am usually extremely introverted and I used to panic at the thought of having to speak to someone I didn't know. I went bright red whenever I was in conversation with anyone and I sat with my back to the audience when it was my time to go up on stage during the school nativity show.

When you travel solo, you put yourself in a position where you have no other choice than to speak to strangers, to network and make new friends. Travelling solo has done absolute wonders for my confidence and it will do the same for yours too. I don't think my family would have believed it if they knew I'd be living at the other side of the world with more confidence than I ever had in the comfort of my hometown, doing work that involves a lot of public speaking. Public speaking? Crazy for a shy girl, right?

Believe it or not, introverts often find travelling solo a lot easier than extroverts might. Extroverts might feel comfortable going out and speaking to new people, but they will find it much more difficult during the times when they have to sit by themselves if they are not already used to this.

TOUR GROUPS: Take the stress away.

If it's your first time travelling solo and you feel worried about meeting new people, I would recommend looking into tour groups. Although travelling in a tour group is not technically solo travelling, periodic guided social experiences can enhance your overall adventure. It will also teach you the best ways to travel, so that next time you're able to do it by yourself with confidence.

The first time I travelled without friends or family, I went with a tour group to Bali, Indonesia. I loved every minute and met some amazing people who I now consider some of my best friends. With an organised tour group, you are guaranteed to meet new people. It takes the stress away from planning everything yourself and you will have so much fun and constant laughter with a group of strangers, who will quickly become amazing friends. I recommend arriving a day before your tour starts and staying a few days after it concludes, if you have the flexibility to do so. Many people from the tour group will usually stay on and visit more areas, so it's fun to be able to do this together. I left on the day that my Bali tour finished and I remember having the biggest F.O.M.O (Fear of missing out) when I saw the others still exploring together.

ACTIVITY CLASSES:
Find friends with similar interests.

If you don't fancy a tour group and want to throw yourself right in there, a good way of meeting new people is by attending classes. There are so many classes from cooking classes, gym classes, yoga, dance, boxing, jujitsu, football and art classes. If you attend classes that you're interested in, you will meet other solo travellers with similar interests. You have already tried something new by travelling solo. Why not also try some new activities that you wouldn't normally think to try in your home country? You never know, you might find yourself a few new hobbies.

The beautiful thing about travelling is you'll find out so much more about yourself because you're always trying out new activities, eating new food and surrounding yourself with new people in new environments.

If you're planning on travelling while working remotely, there are plenty of cafes and co-working spaces around, which provide great opportunities to meet like-minded digital nomads. There are many co-living accommodations which usually include free co-working spaces too. I've stayed in co-working accommodation when I needed a break from the party side of travelling, which was great for my productivity and also for meeting new people.

HOSTELS:
A great way of meeting other solo travellers.

Hostels are a great way of meeting other solo travellers. Many people feel there's a stigma around hostels and think they're unclean and unsafe. With most places, this isn't the case. I've stayed in many gorgeous hostels. You probably wouldn't be able to tell it was a hostel if it wasn't stated on the booking site. You can often book private rooms if you don't want to share with strangers. You will still be able to meet other people if you head down to the pool or check out the bar, they are always very sociable. A friend I met travelling had never stayed in a hostel before because his budget allowed him to book private hotel rooms, but he specifically chose to stay in a hostel this time as he knew he'd be guaranteed to meet people if he chose a sociable hostel.

To ensure the hostel you book is sociable, you should ▣ **look at recent reviews**. Many hostels haven't had any guests since the pandemic, so they may not be as sociable as their photos make it out to be.

You can find a Facebook group for the destination you're visiting and ask for recommendations for sociable accommodation. If you speak to the staff, they will be able to give you information on the best places to go and events that are happening so that you can meet other people. The hostels themselves usually host events to get people networking; these could be night or daytime events. I met a group of friends on a hostel-arranged boat tour that later became travelling companions. The boat trips that hostels arrange are often amazing. The one I did, took us to the most surreal places I've ever been to in my life, I felt like I was in those travel videos you see on YouTube or Instagram—crystal clear lagoons, beaches with sand that feels like you're standing on a bed of flour. Hostels also make the tours a lot of fun because they know everyone wants to socialise. They put on good music, give out drinks and play volleyball on the beach with us.

SOCIAL MEDIA:
Take advantage of the Internet chatter.

Take advantage of social media; meeting people you know online isn't such a crazy thought anymore. Most places you will travel to have a Facebook community group page followed by lots of other solo travellers. Look out for any other girls that might want to meet up or put a post in the group yourself to see if anyone with similar interests would like to meet up. Planned events and meet-ups will get posted in these groups too. You could also check out Instagram locations and hashtags for the area you're visiting, to see if there are any other solo travellers in the area at the time.

Bumble BFF is a great app to find friends with similar interests. I've met a few friends from using this app, it's not just for dating! Social media platforms are great tools, but always use your intuition when connecting with other travellers. Check whether they look like a legit account (tip—always check how old their social media account is), and whether they look like a person you'd get along with.

YOU WILL MAKE FRIENDS IN THE LEAST EXPECTED PLACES. I've gained friends from a passing comment I made in a restaurant, I have one very close group of travel friends, just from a comment shouted down the street after a night out.

My strangest way of meeting friends while travelling solo was… at a petrol station. I was on a very quiet island in the Philippines, with not many other tourists around. I pulled over to fill up my bike and there was an English couple who didn't know how much petrol to put in. I helped them as another three girls pulled into the petrol station. We all got talking and decided to spend the next few days travelling the island together. The next day, as we were on the way to waterfalls that we had planned to visit, we stopped off at the same petrol station and were just about to leave when another group of people pulled over and started talking to us, who then ended up coming along to the waterfalls with us.

I'd gone from solo travelling to being in a group of ten, just by being in the right place at the right time. You don't need to try too hard to make friends, let them come naturally. If you're really struggling to make friends, go and stand at a petrol station on Siquijor island in the Philippines. You never know who you'll meet there! Jokes aside, if you try out a few of the above tips, you'll be sure to meet new people in no time.

You may feel quite desperate or in a rush to make friends when you're on your first ever solo trip. It's completely normal to feel like this. Going to a foreign country alone for the first time is daunting for the majority of people and it definitely was for me. But as you gain more confidence and experience, some of you may find that you don't need to be meeting new people *all* of the time.

For me, it gets tiring when you're travelling for long periods. Sometimes I like to spend days by myself to recharge. I've also found that I prefer travelling to each destination alone and meeting brand new people each time. I've loved the times when I've met people I get along with and we carried on our travels together, but when I stick with the same group of people and then travel to several destinations with them, I feel like I'm not solo travelling anymore. It's *solo* travel that I love the most, because I can go about my days on my own terms, meet new people when I feel like meeting new people and spend time relaxing alone when I feel like I need a break. So, depending on your personality and how long you're travelling, you may not need to put so much pressure on yourself to be meeting new people every day.

By travelling solo, you will meet people from all over the world. You will start to notice that you have friends and contacts from many different countries. When you visit these countries, you will already know someone there that you can meet up with. When I travelled to the Philippines, I ended up meeting two friends that I'd met in Bali a few months earlier. We were on the same island at the same time, so we met up for some day trips and nights out. You'll be surprised at how many people you meet that are from your hometown, even people that you knew of, but you never thought you'd be friends with at home.

When I arrived in the Philippines, I got a message from someone who lived in the same town as me saying that he was going to be in the Philippines within the next week. I arranged to meet up with him and the group of friends he'd made while travelling to other countries in Asia. These people became great friends to travel with—although it's funny as we'd never have arranged to meet up at home, only at the other side of the world. You will also make friends who are a lot older or younger than yourself or friends you consider to be very different from yourself. On one of my solo trips, I made a friend who was ten years older than me and we ended up travelling to several different places together. I found that at home, I stuck to making friends around a similar age range to myself, people who had similar interests to me, but when travelling, you realise that although the friends you meet can be much older, younger, or can come from different backgrounds and have different interests, these people can teach you a lot. They're interesting to hang out with and they can still become lifelong friends.

I know making friends is one of the main worries people have before travelling solo (it definitely was mine!) But trust me when I say, you'll begin as a solo traveller, and you'll come away with a whole new network of friends.

You'll begin as a solo traveller, but you'll come away with a new network of friends.

@elizacroft_

NEED TO KNOW

THE ART OF MINIMALIST PACKING

Why do most girls overpack? That's especially the case when we don't know what to expect. When travelling, you need to adopt a minimalist mindset. You can't bring your whole wardrobe! Don't try to pack a different outfit for every day and every night, there are launderettes available in the majority of places and you'll regret packing so much when you're re-packing your bag every few days. I was surprised when I travelled around South East Asia that there was a laundry lady at every block who would wash all my clothes and return them the next day for little expense. It felt like a luxury.

When I decided to travel full-time with no end date, I took as many clothes with me as I possibly could, only to end up sending most of them home when my family came to visit and leaving another large bag full of clothes for my friend when I moved on from Bali. Now I'm in Thailand and I'm wishing I had given away even more items before I went travelling again. My suitcase is now stored away and I take a small hand luggage bag around with me to travel.

As well as overpacking, another thing us girls tend to do is go shopping before we go on holiday and buy a whole new wardrobe. I've learnt not to do this before travelling. You will end up wearing your favourite outfits repeatedly and clothes can easily get ruined, so don't take any expensive clothes. You will find nobody cares what you look like or how many times you wear the same clothes when you're travelling. So, my best piece of packing advice is to not take clothes that you don't want to see ruined as you can't guarantee that the launderette won't turn your white t-shirts into grey t-shirts or make your shorts feel like they're fit for a small child.

I made the mistake of buying a lot of new clothes when I arrived in Bali. Unfortunately for me, the colour I suit the most is white, so naturally I bought lots of lovely white Bali-style clothes that I thought would look great on my tanned skin. However, my wardrobe now looks like my favourite colour is grey. I'm still yet to find a launderette that will keep my clothes the colour and size that they're supposed to be, but while I'm still on the search for this, the best advice I can give to you is to ◼ **bring cheap clothes that you can lose or ruin.**

HOWEVER, AS MUCH AS I WISH I COULD, I CAN'T PUT ALL THE blame for my clothes being ruined onto the laundrettes. They can't take the blame for me belly-flopping off the bar stools into the beach club pool, fully clothed, on New Year's Eve. Nor can they take the blame for me and my friend, Dee, then having to walk around for the rest of the night in soaking wet-through dresses, with drenched hair and make-up running down our faces while everyone else was dressed up to the nines. Another reason not to bring clothes you don't want ruined—you never know when you'll be swimming fully clothed.

I once went on a sunset dinner date. The sunset was beautiful, but we'd walked too far up the beach. The tide was in and the waves were crashing up against the rocks. There was no other way to get back, so swimming was the only option. Fully clothed. Swimming with my clothes on was becoming a regular thing for me. With my white shorts and t-shirt, my bag held up in the air and the waves pushing me closer to the rocks, I swam until we finally reached a part of the beach where we could get out of the water. Being a guy, he could take his clothes off to ring the water out, but I didn't fancy doing the same and letting the whole beach see me in my underwear. He then drove me straight to dinner, where I walked in with soaked, see-through clothes, hair covered with sea salt and makeup dripping down my face. This was another outfit that got ruined, but I guess it broke the ice on the first date.

The same goes for shoes; if you're hiking up a volcano, you don't want to be in your best trainers because the path up there isn't smoothly tarmacked. For most, you are scrambling up rocks that will turn your shoes black no matter what the weather is like. Or if you're learning how to drive a moped in a cow's field, I'd highly advise you not to wear brand new white trainers as you will need to put your feet down to balance. Can you imagine what I placed my foot into? At least I wasn't in flip-flops. Later, I hung my head in shame as I gave the poor laundress just one of my shoes to clean (I did get most of it off myself before giving it to her, I'm not such a bad person!).

◙ **Packing cubes** are an absolute must to have while travelling. This was another mistake I made when I first travelled—I decided to pack all my clothes separately into my backpack. A lot of the time you'll be having early morning wake-ups and rushing to make your transport on time, so the last thing you want to be doing is pulling everything out of the top of your bag just to find a shirt that is right at the bottom. You can purchase packing cubes and they will be your life savers when travelling. Pack your tops in one, bikinis in another and so on. When you're moving areas every few days you don't want to be unpacking and packing each time, so having them already packed in sections helps.

◼ **Backpack vs Suitcase**. I would say this depends on the type of travelling you're planning to do. The first couple of times I went travelling I went with a backpack, but when my family came out to visit me in Bali, I sent it home with them and kept their suitcase instead, not knowing that one month later I'd be leaving Bali to go backpacking again. I find it easier to travel with a suitcase when I'm travelling long-term with no end date and I know I won't be moving around much, but when I'm travelling for a couple of months, staying in hostels, sleeper buses and moving around a lot, then I prefer to take a *small* backpack.

Before my first ever solo trip, I went shopping for my backpack. I immediately headed for the largest one I could find, which was a big mistake. There's nothing worse than travelling with a huge, heavy bag. ◼ **Travelling with a small backpack means you can use it as hand luggage**, which will save you a huge amount of money on flights. Adding on a checked-in bag adds up to around £20-50 for each flight, so if you're travelling to a few different countries, I'd advise packing light.

If you choose a backpack over a suitcase, I'd recommend buying one with a zip that opens up at the front, so you can open it like a suitcase. This just avoids having to take every single item out each time you want to get one thing. If you pack a lot, then backpacks can be extremely heavy to carry if you're walking long distances. For context, the first time I went travelling, mine weighed 20kg and I felt like I was doing a gym workout every time I lifted it onto my back. However, it's not often you'll be walking long distances. The only time I've found myself doing so is when I was catching a ferry and had to walk down the harbour. Or when my airport transfer in Vietnam dropped me off twenty minutes away from where my hotel was and I had to walk.

If you choose a backpack, you'll be grateful you don't have a suitcase to drag across the sand on the islands. I know a lot of people that have dumped their suitcases halfway through their backpacking trip, but I also know a lot of people who have dumped their backpacks because they find it easier to have a suitcase. My personal choice is a backpack for travelling to multiple areas within a country and a suitcase if travelling to one destination for a short period of time.

So, I've left you with the pros and cons and now the choice is yours!

▣ **Roll up your clothes**. It sounds simple but when you figure out a way where you can make them small and not crease up, it's much easier to pack this way and you will be able to fit more into your bag. The vacuum packs from Amazon are also a game changer if you want to fit more clothes into your bag. Also, remember to mark your luggage, you can buy luggage tags from cheap shops or online. Luggage can sometimes go missing and having your contact details attached will help get it returned to you much quicker.

▣ **A microfibre towel, toothbrush tube and reusable toiletry bottles are useful things to pack**. Having a microfibre towel leaves a lot more space in your bag than packing a normal towel would, and they're much lighter and dry quickly. You never know what bugs might end up in your bathroom, so it's handy to have a tube to keep your toothbrush in; this keeps it clean in your bag too. You can buy reusable toiletry bottles from many places. I got mine from Primark. Rather than carrying huge bottles of every product you own, small bottles will save a lot of space in your bag, keep it lighter and you can also take them in your hand-luggage if you aren't checking in any large bags.

Even if you're going to a scorching hot country, always bring warm clothes. Just one pair of trousers, one hoodie and a pair of trainers will be fine. Long transport journeys with air conditioning can get chilly and you never know, you might decide to climb to the top of a volcano, which could be freezing. When you're travelling to a hot country it can sometimes slip your mind that you might occasionally get cold. For some strange reason, I thought Australia was hot all year round so I only packed summer clothes. I suppose it wasn't as cold as the U.K, but when I arrived after I'd just been in Asia, I found it quite chilly. Luckily, I was visiting my friend who let me live in her clothes for the whole time I was there, otherwise, I would have either needed to make a very expensive shopping trip or frozen to death in the evenings.

Believe it or not, it rains in these hot countries too. A thin rain jacket is a useful thing to have, even if you buy one when you're out there. If you're travelling to a country that has 'rainy seasons,' this won't save you, even as rainy seasons aren't as bad as they sound. Usually, it rains for a few hours every few days, maybe once a day for an hour or so. But when the storms arrive, that's when it can get quite bad.

WHEN I SAY BAD, I MEAN MY WHOLE BEDROOM AND BATHROOM flooded in the newly-built villa I was living in. I called the landlord to help and they came over to mop the water out, then they left. I just had to laugh at this point as I could see the water still coming up from the floorboards, so mopping the water out wasn't any use at all and quite frankly there was nothing I could do apart from go to sleep and hope that when I woke up it would have all dried up, which is what I decided to do. Some would say this wasn't the smartest idea, as it could have been a different story if I woke up to the water rising as high as my bed. But I trusted that Bali storms didn't last that long and I was extremely tired, so I closed my eyes and ignored the problem. It's safe to say, my gut instinct was right this time and I woke up with my room looking like nothing had happened.

Pack a reusable water bottle, this will save you money on water as you'll find many places have re-fill stations. But most importantly, it saves the environment too.

If you're a light sleeper, I'd recommend packing an eye mask and ear plugs. Not everyone is quiet on flights, overnight trains and in hostels. They're a must-have if you want your beauty sleep. I'd also recommend bringing your earphones or a book for any long trips, to keep you entertained.

Depending on where you're travelling to, you may be on long-haul flights which can run over several days. Always remember to pack your toothbrush, face wash/wipes and clean underwear in your hand luggage. Long flights can make you feel unclean and this will keep you feeling so much fresher.

Tampons, girls! This is something I never thought about and not taking any is a mistake you definitely want to avoid if you use them. For most countries I've visited, this hasn't been an issue, but in Asia, make sure you're stocked up on tampons.

You'll rarely find a shop that has them in, unless you want to be paying £20 for a pack of six.

I was searching every shop high and low in Bali. I realised it was a problem for all girls in Asia. There are very few shops that sell them, so you might have to travel a while before you find any. I made the mistake of not bringing any with me and it resulted in my mum shipping a load over from the U.K. Thanks, mum, for paying the very expensive import fees! Months later, I also asked my mum to bring a few more boxes out when she visited me, so that they'd last me until I next came home, I was thinking she would bring around four boxes but she brought about twenty-four. Did she not realise I only have one period per month? They filled up a whole small suitcase and she got stopped at security. The confused Indonesian officer asked her what they were and why she had so many. I didn't realise that I would be leaving Bali so soon after she visited, moving on to travel as a backpacker again and I was stuck with hundreds of tampons that I couldn't fit in my suitcase. I managed to donate a lot of them to friends who were also looking for them. Sanitary towels aren't an issue, but they're not really what you need when you want to be spending your days in a bikini!

Don't worry if you do forget to pack anything. There are always ways around it and plenty of shops available (unless you're on a remote island, then you have no hope). If you can buy it in your own country, you can most likely find something similar in other places too. Unless it's some good English crisp or chocolate. But I suppose you eat healthier when you don't have your usual go-to snacks.

Anyway, as you can see from the many stories I have about my clothes getting lost or ruined, it's not the smartest idea to pack your favourite clothes. The items you'll need to pack will depend on where you're going. Below is a list of what you *could* pack, then a list of what I would pack after half of it's been crossed out. Remember when you're packing, if it's a 'maybe' it's a 'no.'

PACKING LIST

Here's a list of everything that you *could* pack:

Clothes:

◈ Underwear
◈ Bras
◈ Socks
◈ Sleepwear
◈ T-Shirts
◈ Leggings/trousers
◈ Hoodie
◈ Shorts
◈ Swimwear/cover-ups
◈ Dresses
◈ Coats/Jackets
◈ Jeans
◈ Gym wear
◈ Hats/gloves/scarves
◈ Trainers/athletic/ walking shoes
◈ Sandals/flip flops

Accessories:

◈ Jewellery
◈ Belt
◈ Purse
◈ Photos of family/friends
◈ Sunglasses
◈ Glasses
◈ Beach bag/small bag

Toiletries:

◈ Toothbrush
◈ Toothpaste
◈ Shampoo/Conditioner
◈ Face wash
◈ Body wash
◈ Deodorant
◈ Hairbrush
◈ Hair styling tools

- ◈ Moisturiser
- ◈ Face cleanser
- ◈ Sunscreen
- ◈ Insect repellent
- ◈ Tweezers
- ◈ Nail file/clippers
- ◈ Pain killers
- ◈ Medications
- ◈ Sanitary towels/tampons
- ◈ Shaving products
- ◈ Makeup
- ◈ Makeup brushes
- ◈ Contact lenses/solution

Electronics:

- ◈ Mobile phone
- ◈ Phone charger
- ◈ Laptop
- ◈ Laptop charger
- ◈ Plug adaptors
- ◈ Power bank

Carry on:

- ◈ Headphones
- ◈ Eye mask
- ◈ Ear plugs
- ◈ Travel pillow
- ◈ Underwear (long hauls)
- ◈ Face wash/wipes (long hauls)
- ◈ Toothbrush/toothpaste (long hauls)
- ◈ Food/snacks
- ◈ In-flight medications
- ◈ Valuables
- ◈ Notebook/pen
- ◈ Cash
- ◈ Credit cards
- ◈ Passport
- ◈ Visa (if necessary)
- ◈ COVID-related documents/masks
- ◈ Back-up copies of your documents
- ◈ Entertainment— books/playing cards

Here are my essentials, both the mundane obvious stuff, and critical items that saved my ass many times.

Note: I hate the cold. Though there are many lovely places to go in cold climes, most of my travel is to sunny, tropical locations.

Clothes:

- Underwear
- Sleepwear
- T-Shirts ×10
- Shorts ×3
- Dress ×1
- Leggings/trousers ×1
- Bikinis ×4
- Trainers ×1
- Flip Flops ×1

Accessories:

- Sunglasses
- Glasses
- Small purse bag
- Packing cubes

Toiletries:

- Toothbrush
- Hairbrush
- Sunscreen
- Medications
- Sanitary towels/tampons
- Makeup & brushes— (1 foundation powder, 1 mascara, 1 eyebrow liquid, 1 lip gloss)
- Contact lenses

Electronics:

- Mobile phone
- Phone charger
- Laptop
- Laptop charger
- Plug adaptors
- Power bank

Carry on:

- Headphones
- Notebook/pen
- Book
- Cash
- Credit cards
- Passport

You need to adopt a minimalist mindset. You can't bring your whole wardrobe!

@elizacroft_

MUST-HAVE TRAVEL APPS

Wouldn't it be nice if travel could be made simple? Travel isn't always coconuts and beaches; it's a lot of planning, long travel days and adapting to change. I know how overwhelming it may feel at first.

Luckily, there are many travel apps that make our lives a lot easier. From planning, to booking, to help during your trip—downloading these apps will make everything seem simple.

◉ **Maps.me/Google Maps**—You can use maps.me with no internet connection, so it's a good idea to download this before you go, in case you find yourself in a situation without Wi-Fi/data. Just make sure to pre-download the map of the country while you still have an Internet connection. As well as navigating where you're going, Google Maps can also be used to pinpoint places on the map, which can be helpful when planning your itinerary.

◉ **Currency Converter**—This app is a godsend when you visit a new country. There's nothing worse than not knowing how much you're being charged for something, whether you're being ripped off or whether whatever you're buying is reasonably priced. Simply open this app and type in the amount you're being charged and you'll see it converted to the currency you understand.

◉ **Google Translate**—Another useful app just to make life a little easier when travelling. Most people I've met travelling speak fluent English but there are a lot of people who don't. This app is handy for the moments when the person you're communicating with doesn't understand what you're trying to say, or vice versa.

◘ **Hostelworld**—This is a great app for those of you looking to stay in cheap hostels. It has options for places all over the world!

◘ **Booking.com**—This is the app I use to book the majority of my accommodation. You don't need to use this app if you've found another you prefer, but I advise sticking to the same booking app as they tend to give you discounts and rewards for being loyal.

◘ **Tripscout**—This app is extremely useful for planning your trips. You simply choose the country you want to visit and it will provide you with all you need to know, from the best food places to activities and experience days, accommodation recommendations and itineraries to follow.

◘ **Rome2rio**—This is one of the most useful travel apps out there. It will help you find the easiest, best and most cost-effective route to any destination.

◘ **Transport apps**—It's useful to download an app to order taxis from. This will save you time, you'll know the taxi company is safe and you'll know you're paying the correct price. Sometimes they might give you discounts for using the app as well. Which app to download will depend on the country you're visiting. For example, for Europe and USA, it could be Uber. For Asia, it could be Grab.

◘ **Duolingo**—This is an amazing app to learn the language of the country you're visiting. Even if it's just the basics, the locals will appreciate your effort. Although a few countries aren't listed on the app, most of them are!

◨ **Nord VPN**—This is the VPN server I use for my phone and laptop so that I still get access to everything I would use back home in the U.K. It doesn't have to necessarily be a VPN from this company, but it's useful to have a VPN if travelling long-term. If you're only travelling for a short period, I probably wouldn't bother getting one.

◨ **TravelSpend**—This is a great app to track how much you're spending on your travels so that you can ensure you're sticking to your budget.

◨ **Google Photos**—Keep all your photos backed up. If anything happens to your phone while travelling, you won't lose all the memories that you can look back on.

◨ **GoOut!**—Check if the country you're in has any promotion deal apps or Instagram accounts. It's an amazing app to show you the food deals in each area of the country. I used the 'GoOut!' app while I was in Bali and saved a lot of money on my food.

◨ **Been**—Easily keep track of all the countries you visited; see what percentage of the world you've seen and how much you've still got left to experience!

PHOTOGRAPHER OR NOT

Whether you're a professional photographer or not, the photos you capture while travelling will be sure to upgrade your Insta' feed (or your camera roll if social media isn't your vibe). While I strongly believe in living in the moment, it's great to capture some cool travel photos to look back on when you get home (that's if you ever decide to go home).

I'm no photographer, although I did do GCSE photography at school if that counts! But I've figured out some little tips for taking photos during my time solo travelling. One 'difficult' thing about solo travelling is not having anyone to take your photo if you decide to go sightseeing on your own (what a first-world problem). Most of the time you'll have made friends who also want to go to the same places as you do, but for times when you're on your own, ◘ **it's handy to have a tripod** if you find a cool photo spot.

◘ **GoPros** are great to use for underwater photos. It's not a necessity to have one, so don't go splashing out if you can't afford it, just for the sake of a few underwater snaps. Save your money for the experiences when you get there! You'll most likely meet a friend travelling who has a GoPro anyway, so you can always use theirs. Activity companies usually have one too. I took a GoPro travelling with me, accidentally sent the charger back to the U.K with my sister and I haven't cared enough to go and look for another one yet, as I've managed to get by using other people's. Although I should probably buy, it's shown me that you can still get underwater photos without one. Don't use waterproof phone cases as an alternative to a GoPro, I've used them in the past in the pool and they've been great, but my sister put hers in the sea to capture some videos of dolphins and it broke straight away. It cost a lot of money to fix, but we still managed to save the cool dolphin videos.

You can also use your photos and videos to make ■ **longer videos or vlogs** about your travels. This way, you will be able to watch back on all your adventures. You can even publish them on YouTube as a lot of people will be interested and inspired by your travels! Presets also look great on travel photos, you can buy these from Lightroom or sites like Etsy. I don't mean to pitch my own product here, but I also have my own preset collection (you can find these through the links on my social media accounts), which are specifically made for travel photos.

Another way to keep memories of your adventures is by journaling. I highly recommend ■ **taking a journal** with you and writing down everything that happened each day. Sometimes I forget about the funny stories or crazy adventures I've been on, so I love reading back on my journal every so often.

To get the ■ **best scenery photos,** you want to aim to get to your destination early in the morning. The lighting is best at this time and there are usually no crowds so a lot of the time you'll have the place to yourself, which makes it easier not having people in the background of your photos. I also noticed that wildlife is out early in the morning.

One last tip on this section—■ **Remember to put your camera away!** When we visit beautiful places, it's normal to want to take a few photos to capture the moment, but take some time away from the camera to appreciate the views, look at where you are and notice the feelings you get when seeing these stunning places.

SOAKING UP THE CULTURE

We travel to assimilate culture. It's always nice to research the culture before you travel to a new country. To understand other cultures, you have to make an effort to learn why traditions are important to people and understand their identity.

Create a little bit of cultural curiosity to see things from their eyes, learn a little about how they live, what food they eat and maybe even learn some basic phrases of their language. There may be some things you don't agree with and you may at first experience culture shock, you will start to understand the reasoning for other cultures doing whatever it is they are doing. Indulging in a foreign culture when you travel will alter your concept of 'normal'. It will show you how we have picked up a great deal of our subconscious behaviour and belief from our environment—stuff that we consider 'normal' and it can show you ways in which you can change some of that.

People everywhere appreciate it when you make an effort to learn the basics of their language. Unfortunately, some people in some countries will try to charge you more if they see you're a tourist. But if you know a little of their language, they may realise you're not visiting for the first time and they'll probably charge you the normal rate.

I would suggest ▣ **looking a little into the laws of the country** you're visiting. Some countries have some very unique rules. Did you know it's illegal to leave the house without underwear in Thailand? I'm not sure how anyone would know, but be sure to pack enough underwear so you don't have to have any awkward conversations with your family to tell them the reason for your arrest.

I recommend ◼ **trying some of the local food** wherever you are, it's always tasty. Be careful with street food. It can be some of the best food you'll ever taste, but make sure it's cooked properly, otherwise you'll end up feeling sick for the next week or so. The accommodation I'm staying in right now is just over the road from a street market, so I've spent every evening eating Asian cuisine for less than £2, and so far, I haven't had any sickness problems. If the food looks like it's been sat there for hours with flies buzzing around, it probably has. If the food looks hot, it's constantly going around in the pan and there's a queue of people there, it's good street food. If you ask to keep the chilli out of the food in certain countries, your dish will most likely still be spicy, so you won't need extra unless your taste buds are resilient.

You may start to experience cultural exhaustion. It's hard to live differently for so long when you're away from the comforts of your own culture. You'll probably have some days where you just need some home comforts, so you'll head out to find a western-style restaurant where you can eat pizzas and burgers.

Always respect the locals and their culture. It's extremely interesting and eye-opening to see how other cultures live compared to yourself in your home country. Different cultures will expand your knowledge and understanding of the world we live in. You will get to know their religious and cultural rules and their days of celebration.

'Nyepi' is a fascinating festival in Bali, a day of complete silence, reserved for self-reflection. You aren't allowed out of your home. Lights and sounds must be turned off and all shops and restaurants are closed, but a few days before this religious day there are celebrations all over the island. I love to experience cultural celebrations as you can learn a lot from them. Local people put a lot of effort into these events and the high energy is intense.

> *I MET AN INDONESIAN MAN WHO WORKED IN A SURF SHACK ON A beach and I asked him what time it was. Instead of looking at his phone or watch, he looked up at the sun and told me it was around 11am. I was extremely surprised he knew this. I asked him to check the time digitally. I was shocked; it was 10:50 am. He told me that he always tells the time by looking at the sun and I think this is a beautiful way to live, where the only concept of time you have is by being with nature.*

I've found a lot of people who live in Asia don't have much concept of time, they don't pay much attention to how long things take. Everything happens at a slow pace. A lot of restaurants in Asia take a while to make food, but after living in the Far East for a while, I've learnt to live the slow-paced lifestyle and I now much prefer it to the fast-paced life we live in the Western world.

I love making friends with locals. It allows connections between different cultures and your new friends will show you hidden gems, teach you their way of living and maybe even cook you some of their homemade food or take you to a traditional ceremony.

> *I WENT TO A QUIET ISLAND IN THE PHILIPPINES WHICH WAS known as the 'healing island'. I'd been recommended to visit a healer there, whether I believed in the healing process or not. I wasn't planning to go but I ended up driving past a house with a healing sign, so I went in. It was an unusual experience, that included blowing and whispering behind my head. Whatever*

she did, she managed to heal the pain in my upper back and
neck that I'd had for four years, since I'd been involved in a
car crash. I was hoping that she'd be able to heal the injury I'd
gotten a few days before from swinging off a rope swing into a
waterfall, but unfortunately, this one lasted a few more months.
Maybe I was trying my luck.

This same healer invited me and my friends to a fiesta that
was taking place in her village the following day. I was also
lucky to meet a local family when I lived in Bali and they invited
me to their niece and nephew's 'Tooth Filing Ceremony'. The
Tooth Filing Ceremony marks the time when a Hindu teenager
is ready to enter the world of adulthood. It must be performed
once in someone's lifetime and is one of the most important
religious ceremonies in Bali. The ceremony is undertaken to
remove impurities in the human body and soul. I feel so grateful
to have been able to experience this. I felt truly immersed in the
Balinese culture and it was eye-opening for sure.

Once you've familiarised yourself with the culture and the
way that the locals live, I'd also advise that you familiarise yourself with the indigenous animals' way of living too. Depending
on which country you go to, you might just need to accept
that you'll have a pet lizard that lives on your bedroom wall.
You might encounter monkeys that roam the streets and try to
steal your food. Let me tell you though, monkeys aren't as cute
as they look, those beasts are crafty! Never look a monkey in
the eye, keep your possessions close and you'll be fine. I can't
say that having your possessions zipped away in your bag can
be much help though; I visited a monkey sanctuary and had
a monkey sit on my shoulder. I was too busy smiling at the
camera to notice that he'd unzipped my bag and taken out my
sunglasses. They were only £3 from Primark.

Going into a situation you've never been in and a country you know nothing about allows your mind to expand and see what else is out there. It allows you to create your own perspective on the country instead of having a perception based on what other people tell you or what you see in the media. When you visit a country, it's not just that specific culture you'll learn about. You'll meet people from all over the world who will tell you about the cultures they grew up in and how it was for them.

I know that I'm extremely lucky to have been brought up in the U.K., where we have endless opportunities, and when I hear stories from people who have grown up in less developed countries, I get an immeasurable feeling of gratitude. Some of the people you meet on your travels come from nothing and some people still have nothing to this day, yet they manage to find joy in every single day. Seeing with your own eyes, how other humans live, will help you understand that materialistic things do not matter, small problems that we perceive as big problems do not matter. Nothing matters other than the feeling of happiness inside of you and your loved ones.

An important aspect of respecting the culture is considering our environmental impact, so that we travel as responsibly and sustainably as possible. Every little thing makes a difference; pick up plastic on the beach, turn the air conditioning off before you leave the room, tell the maid that your room doesn't need cleaning every day, re-use towels, re-use your water bottle, take public transport as much as you can or walk or cycle to places not too far. Pay attention to which companies you book with, are they environmentally friendly? Does the elephant sanctuary treat the animals correctly? Although you might be tempted by an iced latte from Starbucks, try to eat and shop at places where the food is locally sourced, as this helps out the local business owners.

I recently just ticked a huge bucket list item off my list. I say huge as they were 39 ft long, but also because this has been at the top of my bucket list for years. I swam with whale sharks which was probably the best experience I've ever had in my life. Although it was scary getting in the water at first as I could see their fins popping up, when I got comfortable, it was the most magical experience. We swam with three whale sharks!

Sometimes I'd look behind me and there would be one of them swimming right towards me. We kept having to swim away as you can't get too close for ethical reasons. Although it was a once-in-a-lifetime experience, you have to make sure the company you use is ethical. I avoided a certain area as I'd heard that it was overcrowded and people touch them. To ensure the company treats the whale sharks correctly, please do your research; they mustn't be fed as this is unnatural and you should keep a distance of at least six metres. Whale sharks don't mind humans being around. They will swim away if they get uncomfortable, so you shouldn't follow them when they do this.

Try to give back to the communities in the places you visit as much as possible by maintaining sustainable travel. Volunteering is also a good way of giving back and providing positive change to communities you pass through. Giving to others is an amazing feeling for both parties and it creates changes for those who need it the most. You will enjoy your experience more knowing that you're having a positive impact on the environment and the communities around you.

Many volunteering projects around the world would be grateful to receive your help. You can sign up to sites for volunteering opportunities that return the favour by providing you with accommodation and food, such as *World Packers* or *Work Away*. My friends recently took part in two weeks of volunteering for four hours, four days a week with one of these companies. They had all their accommodation and food paid for and were able to explore the country in their spare time. There are plenty of opportunities like this available all over the world.

For me, culture is an important part of my travel experiences. Each time I experience it, it makes my heart fill up just a little more.

Through culture, I've gained most of my knowledge of the world. I understand why people have different beliefs and different ways of life. I've learned a lot from interacting with local people, networking with other travellers from different countries and making the effort to indulge in food and events that I wouldn't experience in my home country.

ALTHOUGH I'VE HAD SEVERAL GREAT EXPERIENCES, THERE'S been one man in particular that has impacted my life through culture. His name is Lan. I met Lan while working in Thailand. He is a guide from a small village in the Chiang Mai jungle.

Lan is the most talkative person I have ever met and he will say out loud anything that comes to his mind. The first time I met him, I was sat in the car with him on a two-hour drive. He made a comment about my acne, which I have struggled with for ten years. He told me that all I needed to do was put honey, lemon, turmeric and aloe vera on my face and it would disappear. I thought he was being an arsehole. After ten years of trying everything I could, why did this man think he could fix my skin with his jungle-made remedy? I was pretty sensitive to his comment at the time, as my acne was and is my biggest insecurity.

After my first night sleeping over in the jungle with my group of new friends, he pulled up some turmeric from the ground and told the whole group that this is what I should use to fix my face. Now I really thought he was being an arsehole. My sensitive-self took myself for a 'nature wee' in the middle of the jungle and burst into tears. Other people had told me about this man, I wondered why they all loved him so much.

Fast forward to the next month, I was due to visit the jungle again and I was praying that he wouldn't talk about my acne this time, but I tried to go with an open mind. As I thought, it was one of the first things he spoke about, but this time, I accepted his help as he hand-picked me all the ingredients for this treatment he talked about. The only thing missing was the honey.

A couple of days later, I was sat in a restaurant that Lan knew I visited. He called me to say he was outside. I walked out of the restaurant to see him standing across the road next to his motorbike. He walked over with a huge smile and a water bottle that he'd filled and labelled 'wild honey.' At this moment my heart burst. He had been so thoughtful and selfless by going out of his way to help me.

From then, I looked forward to the times I would spend in the jungle with Lan. He taught me a lot. He showed me how he grew up in the jungle—he taught me to cook using coal and fire, he showed me how he ate ants that tasted like lemon (they really do), how he could be so friendly with the spiders in the jungle and how he could dig up a tarantula from a hole in the ground and hold it safely with his hands (do not try this yourself—Lan is a jungle man and knows what he is doing). He even got me over my fear of spiders and now I can sit comfortably with one crawling over my face. He knew what every leaf in the jungle could do—you could blow bubbles out of some, create fake blood out of others and make 'jungle tattoos' out of yet another, by using the leaf sap and dirt from the ground.

He always drove us to a local village where the 'Karen tribe' live. He showed us how they lived off very little, although the people I got to know were some of the happiest and kindest people I've ever met.

Lan and I are complete opposites. I tell him he's crazy, but a good kind of crazy. He gave me the nickname 'phuh-ying reab-roi' which translates in Thai to 'neat lady'—meaning I'm calm and patient.

One thing that means a lot to Lan is family. He speaks to his mother every day and each time I see him he checks to see whether I have spoken to my parents that day. He loves to say hi to my parents when I call them. After a call with my dad, I looked over at Lan and his eyes were filled with tears.

"What's wrong?" I asked.

"It just makes me so happy to hear you tell your father you love him. Always tell your family you love them."

I knew from this that Lan had a big heart. He cared so much about other people. Even when he had been in a serious motorbike accident the day before and couldn't walk properly, he still showed up to trek two hours into the jungle for me and my group. He said he couldn't let me down, although he should have been in the hospital.

Lan once invited me to go to Wat Doi Suthep, in Chiang Mai province. After we ate crispy pork at his favourite local Thai restaurant, he drove me up through the hills to the temple on the back of his old motorbike, which had no wing mirrors and was questionably unsafe. When we arrived, it was almost closing time, so we ran up the 309 steps to make it on time. He showed me the temple and the view over Chiang Mai city. We watched fireworks going off and planes landing at the airport. He told me he hadn't been there in ten years, and the last person he brought to this temple was his mother. He then gave me a small gift and told me that whenever I needed help or felt sad, I could hold this gift to my heart and it would help.

Lan showed me that other people always needed it more than we do. He reminded me how beautiful every single person in this world was. He taught me to live with simplicity, kindness and happiness. You know someone is a good person when you come away from being in their company feeling nothing but grateful. Lan is one of these people.

"As the traveller who has once been from home is wiser than he who has never left his doorstep, so a knowledge of one other culture should sharpen our ability to scrutinize more steadily, to appreciate more lovingly, our own."

Margaret Mead—Anthropologist

*Never look
a monkey
in the eye.*

I CAN'T AFFORD IT

L eaving your secure job to go travelling on the other side of the world seems daunting, right?

How do you overcome your legitimate and compelling fears? I was paralysed with fear and indecision before deciding to make the leap. There were several key intuitions that brought me clarity in making my decision to get going.

Have you ever thought that you might not have to leave your job completely? Try asking your employer if you can have ▣ **unpaid leave** so you can have a once-in-a-lifetime opportunity. You'll be surprised at how many employers have a nice side to them. ▣ **Sabbatical leave or gap years** are options. If this doesn't work and you do have to leave your job, it isn't all so bad and don't let this be the reason to stop you. You'll be robbing yourself of experiences that could be life-changing.

Asking yourself what your values are will help you with the choices you will make. Do you value security and commitment more or do you value adventure and freedom more? Neither path is right nor wrong. It all comes down to you and your own values.

If you decide to leave your corporate job, you'll probably have all sorts of different emotions. I've left jobs to go travelling a few times, so I know how overwhelming the feeling is! Ask yourself now, what's the worst that could happen? You run out of money? You will find another job, or believe it or not, you can work while travelling. Sometimes putting yourself in uncomfortable positions can end up being the push you need to seek out new opportunities.

The first time I went travelling, I quit my job but I knew that I would eventually just go back home and find another job, so there was very little pressure for me to have a whole load of savings or another source of income. I knew that as soon as I got back home, I would start earning money again. However, this time I did the same thing. I quit my job, but I was full of fear and felt a lot of pressure because I knew that I wasn't going to go back home to get another job. It felt uncomfortable, but being in a corporate job wasn't an option for me anymore. It didn't fulfil me and I had a burning desire to try out something different, to go down a path that was unfamiliar to anything I'd ever tried before.

I'm not saying everyone should take the same path as me. If your corporate job aligns with your values, if it makes you happy and brings you purpose, you are extremely lucky to have found that. Remember that it always comes down to what you view as success, not what other people's ideas of success are. It isn't about what your life looks like to others, it's about how it feels for you.

Everybody defines success in their own way. Define what it is for you and take the action to get there. When we see success as something we can design ourselves, we stop comparing our lives to those of others. We set ourselves up for failure when we try to be successful according to other people's expectations. Success is the ability to reach *your* goals in life, that are meaning and fulfilling to *you*. There is no single right way to be successful, so long as what you're doing in life brings you happiness and purpose.

SAVING TO TRAVEL

If you plan to leave your job, plan your budget before you quit. Your expenditure will depend on where you're going and for how long. Working out how much you'll need to take will help you figure out how much you'll have to save each month. If for example, you can afford to put an extra £100 per month towards your travel savings, add this up until you reach your estimated budget and this will determine the time frame in which you can plan to travel. One useful tip to make sure you stick to your plan and don't keep dipping into your savings to spend it on nights out, is to set up a separate savings account specifically for your travel savings. Before you know it, you'll have enough saved up to jet off!

SAVING DURING TRAVELLING

One extremely frustrating mistake I made before travelling was not getting a card that avoids foreign transaction fees. It only seems like small fee amounts at first but they build up quite quickly. I recommend getting a ■ **Revolut, Starling, Wise** or **Monzo card**. This is safer than carrying your main bank card around as you'll always have a backup if one gets lost or stolen.

It's also extremely easy to forget to take your bank card out of the ATM. In a lot of places, your money comes out before your card and you have to click a button to get your card back. When you're not used to this, it's very easy to take your money and walk off, forgetting about your bank card. If you forget, good luck getting it back. I have many friends who have left their cards in ATMs. They were told that any cards that got left in there were cut up within a few hours. I once left my card in the machine but luck must have been on my side that day, as a lady came running after me with my card in her hand. There are some kind people in this world.

There are also ways to save yourself money while you're travelling. You should ▣ **walk to places** if you can, although it's tempting to hop in cheap taxis everywhere, these are other expenses that can quickly build up. Remember to never walk anywhere alone in the dark though, this is when you make exceptions for the taxi fees. Depending on which country you visit, ▣ **cooking yourself** will usually work out cheaper than eating out, plus it can be healthier too. It's easy to get into bad eating habits when travelling, so cooking your own food will help you keep track of what you're putting into your body. While on the subject of food, I'd recommend always keeping emergency snacks on you if you get hungry often as I do. You never know when your transport will be delayed or if you're going to an area with no shops in sight.

Does anyone else notice that they spend money more freely when they're on holiday? It's like our brains think that because it's foreign money, it's not real money. You can probably get away with doing that on a one-week holiday, but if you spend like that while travelling long-term, you'll soon find yourself out of pocket. So, ▣ **don't spend money on things that you don't need**. You'll find this saves a lot of money!

When people think of travelling, they think of it being go-go-go all the time. You are allowed to have relaxed days on the beach or exploring a city. For some of your travelling time, try ▣ **doing all the free stuff** like watching sunsets or finding waterfalls, which will save you some money as well.

Another way of saving money is to ▣ **not eat in tourist areas**. Speak to the locals and see where they like to eat or Google some places outside of the busy centre and you'll find they're a lot less expensive than in the main areas. I mentioned this point in the 'Must-Have Travel Apps' section, but it's a good one, so I'll say it again—you should check if the area you're in has any ▣ **food promo deal apps or Instagram accounts**. In Bali for example, there's an app called 'Go Out!' that shows you all the promotion deals for each day of the week.

▣ **Haggle with the locals** to see if you can strike a bargain. Haggling is negotiating the price, which is commonly done in many countries. You will soon find out whether it's considered normal to do this in the country you're in. For example, it's not commonly known to haggle prices in shops in the U.K, but in Asia, it's more common than not. It can feel quite uncomfortable doing this at first, especially when you don't know what a reasonable price is for the item in their currency, but you'll get used to it quite quickly. However, remember to be fair with the price, the locals work hard to provide the items or services you're purchasing.

Another money tip is to ▣ **always have cash on you**. Don't keep too much on you at once, but you'll find some places don't take card, so it's always useful to have cash handy. When I arrived in the Philippines, I was shocked to find that not one place took card, not even the supermarkets.

▣ **Make sure the cash you have is the correct currency.**

I TRAVELLED TO CROATIA WITH MY SISTER AND WE DIDN'T REALISE we'd run out of Croatian kuna until we had to get on a long coach journey, but we did have some euros with us and were told that Croatia normally accepts these too. After around thirty minutes of driving, the ticket man came over to us. We realised we couldn't pay on card and we only had euros left which he refused to take.

"You both need to get off at the next stop," he said abruptly.

I felt like a naughty school girl who was about to get kicked out of class. Two hours passed and the driver still hadn't stopped the coach for us to get off. He came back to us after a while with a big grin on his face and said, "I'll take the euros."

All along he knew he could accept euros, but he decided that at the beginning of the coach journey he was going to make things difficult for people. At least we didn't get dumped in the middle of nowhere without money or a phone signal.

If you're truly travelling on a tight budget, you need to ■ **think about what you're spending right from the start**. I made the mistake of eating in fancy cafés for the first few months, which I didn't think were that bad because they were similar prices to what I paid in the U.K. I watched my savings slowly run out and I knew I had to start thinking about my budget and eat at local places where I could get a main meal for £1.80. I don't know why I didn't do this from the start. The local restaurants were nicer than the majority of these fancy cafes!

If you are truly serious about saving money to travel, you will have to ■ **make some sacrifices**. Sell your belongings, open a travel savings account, cut down on bad spending habits, cancel subscriptions, eat out less and spend less money on alcohol, because that's how it all adds up. It won't be easy, but you will get the most rewarding feeling when you eventually achieve your savings goal.

I once listened to a travel podcast and the speaker made a statement that stuck with me: "It's more about having the courage than having the money. There are a lot more people who travel who have no money, but instead, have the courage."

The majority of people I've met on my travels had very little money, but they believed they could find a way to make it work and they did. One way to force yourself to save money is to book the flight; if nothing is booked, you can back out of your plans easily and you'll be more likely to find excuses as to why you haven't been able to save enough money.

WORK AND TRAVEL

Wouldn't it be nice to get paid while you travel? This is a possibility for you. The majority of people I've met while travelling are digital nomads, who are on the road and earning money to enable them to carry on travelling. However, this isn't the only way to travel. As discussed earlier, you could just save up money before you go, if working while you travel doesn't appeal to you.

There are many different options these days. Have a look at ◙ **remote job sites**. There are jobs out there that will be exactly like your 'normal' job, but you won't have to work in the same office all day every day. Instead, you will have the freedom to choose; you can work on the beach if you like, from the bottom of a ski slope, from a café in your hometown. I even have a friend who's worked from a hot air balloon in Cappadocia, (but let's be serious, was he actually working or just doing it for the 'gram?).

The world is your oyster when you have this rare thing called location freedom. Aside from remote jobs, other options for working online are building up a ■ **side business** until it reaches a point where you can afford to leave your full-time job, or you could use a skill you have to start ■ **freelance work**. Google, YouTube, LinkedIn, search remote work Facebook groups—I'm sure you will find something out there in this ever-evolving online industry.

So you might be wondering, what is a digital nomad? A digital nomad is someone who can perform their occupation entirely online from anywhere in the world. All you need is an internet connection and a laptop or mobile phone. As the amount of people who are falling in love with travel is growing quickly, so is the digital nomad community. There are countless people looking for location independence, with the ability to work under their own desired conditions.

Being a digital nomad isn't for everyone and it has its advantages and disadvantages. To find out whether it could be something you'd enjoy, ask yourself the following questions:

- ◈ Am I comfortable working with a laptop/technology?
- ◈ Does changing your work environment every so often appeal to you?
- ◈ Do I like the idea of having to make my own routine?

The disadvantage of being a digital nomad is that you have to create self-motivation. That can require a lot of hard work and dedication depending on which route you take. If you work for yourself as a freelancer, for example, you have no guaranteed income and no sick or holiday pay. You may have to sacrifice having a stable income and accept the fact you will be earning a low income, if any, at the start of building up this kind of career. However, the potential long-term income from working for yourself has no cap, you could make a lot more than an employment job if you were to keep consistent with it. If you don't fancy becoming a freelance digital nomad or working for yourself, there are plenty of remote working jobs like online English teaching or customer service roles. Being a digital nomad comes with constant ups and downs, changes and challenges. You will need to get good at adapting to new environments and get used to saying goodbye to the new friendships and relationships you've made, over and over again.

In the section on disadvantages, I also wanted to mention the comments you will most likely receive from other people when you first start working online. People who are not familiar with the online workspace will not understand why you'd want to take this route and they'll probably tell you everything online is a scam. These people could well be family members or friends who mean well and want to look out for you but they'll have no knowledge or experience in the online workspace.

Try not to let other people's comments pull you away from trying something new and try not to let it affect your belief that you could make this work. You don't have any responsibility to tell anyone what you're working on if you prefer to work without involving others. I didn't tell anyone at my corporate job about my online work, because I knew it was unfamiliar to many people and I didn't want to spend time answering questions from people who wouldn't be interested. Instead, I answered the only question that came up again and again: "What are you going to do about getting a job?"

I didn't tell anyone that I didn't want a *job* (or at least the type of job they were thinking of). I just said that I'd figure it out. Even now, when I've been working online for a few years, I still get people asking when I'm going to find a 'proper job'.

I WON'T FORGET THE TIME WHEN I FIRST STARTED WORKING online, I had all of these scam comments thrown at me and I even had a Facebook status written about me by a girl in the year above me at school. I remember reading the Facebook status and seeing all her friends' comments, quoting things that I had posted online in regards to my online work. Unfortunately, I let this get to me for a few days, I blocked all of the girls who supported her status with likes and comments and I blocked everyone else I knew this girl was friends with. I then deleted any posts I'd made in the past about working online, I cried and I completely took myself off social media for a few days.

After speaking with a few friends and thinking hard about these comments, I realised that these girls just weren't familiar with online work. It wasn't a common thing around the area we lived in. The girls must have also had some insecurities to talk badly about other people, because no one happy within themselves will go out of their way to hurt other people, especially publicly. When I think back to times when I made a negative comment about someone, it was usually in moments when I didn't feel happy within myself. I've had my own insecurities, which triggered me to make the comment. Your words about others are a reflection of yourself.

Thankfully, this period of upset and setback only lasted a few days and I then used it as motivation to push harder than ever to make working remotely work out for me. It became clear that working remotely while travelling was what I wanted and it was the direction I was going to head in, no matter what comments I got thrown at me. You are going to get negative comments about working online, but don't let these set you back. Use them to push you forward instead. When you start to change, other people will become uncomfortable, but you'll need to become comfortable with this happening.

If you can push aside the few challenges, becoming a digital nomad has endless advantages.

You're not tied to one location.

You can work from wherever you want and also whenever you want.

You can plan your work around your day instead of planning your day around your work.

There are no long commutes to work or sitting in traffic jams twice a day.

If you don't like the cold winter months, you can choose to work in a hotter country during that time. You will gain experience and knowledge by working around other digital nomads and you will become inspired by new environments and the people you meet from all around the world.

Do you value security and commitment more, or do you value adventure and freedom more?

@elizacroft_

I've found that starting in any sort of remote role can help you find your passion and what it is that you love. I first started working online in 2019 as an online travel agent. After one and a half years I realised that I didn't enjoy putting so many hours into something I wasn't extremely passionate about. Although I loved to travel, I didn't enjoy booking holidays for other people (maybe I was slightly jealous that they were the ones going on holiday and not me).

I then joined an online educational platform that taught me different ways to earn money online, how to invest and how to grow a mindset that would get me to where I wanted to be. I'm still a member of this community. Joining a platform like this where I've been surrounded by mentors who push me to improve and a community that cheers on every success, was the move I needed to make to find out how I can make my dream life a reality. I highly recommend having a mentor for whatever area of your life you want to improve—whether this is business, personal development/mindset, finance, health and fitness or a hobby you want to make improvements with. Having a mentor can accelerate your learning and development far quicker than trying to tackle things alone.

The main path I decided to take was to build an online e-commerce business. I built this up for ten months before eventually being able to afford to leave my nine-to-five office job.

While in Bali, my account disappeared, stopped working, taken away. Whatever the reason was, it was outside of my control. I was devastated as I'd worked so hard at building this into something good.

However, if this hadn't happened, I wouldn't have sat down with pen and paper, brainstorming other ideas on how to make enough money to carry on travelling. One of the simplest ways I found to earn money was to teach English online.

I most likely wouldn't have thought about writing this book if I hadn't found myself in a situation in which I had to think creatively. That being said, I didn't write this book to make money. I cannot guarantee that my book will get even one sale (minus the sale from my mum).

I wrote this book with the hope to inspire other women to face their fears, leave situations they're not happy with, have faith in themselves, take the leap and explore the world. Travel has inspired me in many ways, it has been my greatest teacher and it's brought me so much happiness. I hope it does the same for many others.

Trying different online work opportunities has enabled me to develop skills I never knew I had, it's increased my confidence in my abilities and my knowledge of how to work for myself. From working online, I am now surrounded by like-minded individuals and the majority of them are working towards becoming digital nomads too. If you are thinking of becoming a digital nomad then it'd be great if you could find a community or an environment with other people who are on a similar path, as this will progress your skills and provide you with a higher level of motivation.

I was once asked a question by a follower on Instagram, "Do you feel guilty for not being focused on building a career?"

When I first read this question, I laughed and I was confused as to what this person meant. This person asked an innocent question and most likely didn't mean it in a hurtful or offensive way. But from this question, I came to realise two things. The first was that each individual person perceives 'building a career' as something different. Some people might believe building a career is going to university and then getting a job to work your way up the corporate ladder, whereas others might believe that building a career is starting your own business. Neither one of these are wrong and there are many other options for what building a career may look like, but these two are the main ones that come to my mind.

The second thing I realised was that people don't know what my normal day-to-day life looks like. That's because I don't post every moment of my life on Instagram. I only post the highlights of my life, as most people do. I think people who post about their bad days and their insecurities are extremely brave and inspiring. I don't post the highlights of my life to try and act out a fake life that I want people to think I'm living. These highlights are very much real, authentic and they are small doses of what happens in my life. But on my bad days, I just don't *feel* like posting and I don't think people want to see what my bad days look like. If you don't want to post about the days that aren't so great, you don't have to. If you do want to post about your bad days because you think it could help others deal with their issues, as they compare themselves to the unrealistic life acted out of Instagram, then go right ahead. It's up to us what we post on our social media platforms, but it's also up to us to remember that what we see on other people's Instagram feeds is only a tiny snippet of the reality of their lives.

Although I don't post about my bad days on Instagram, I'll be transparent in this book and I can confirm that not every day is a good day when travelling. As I'm writing this, it's 32 degrees with clear blue skies outside and I'd much rather be lying by the pool soaking up the sun, but I know my main priority is to finish this book. As much as I'd love to be by the pool, I love getting lost in writing and I love talking about travel, so I wouldn't want to change what I'm doing right now.

The person who asked me this question hadn't seen me working twelve-hour days in my bedroom trying to 'build my career' (I don't work this much every day, by the way). They hadn't seen the days when I dealt with a lot of stress and headaches while trying to figure out a way to keep money coming in after I quit my corporate job and decided that I now had to rely on myself to generate an income. They hadn't seen the days where I felt homesick, missing the comforts of home and the people I love for so long, or the days where I feel extremely lonely because contact with people at home has drifted much more than I thought it would, or the days where I'm sick while being alone in a foreign country and all I can wish for is to be at home in my own bed with my mum to look after me, (no matter how old you get, you always want that one person there who would usually look after you).

The fact they hadn't seen this side of a 'living your best life' kind of life wasn't the fault of the person who asked me the question. It was an innocent assumption that my everyday life looks something like sunbathing on the beach with a coconut in hand seven days a week. So the answer to this person's question is that I don't feel guilty for not building a career, because, for me, I am. It might look a little different to what society deems to be the correct way to build a career, but becoming a digital nomad could potentially be the best, but most challenging, career-building I'll ever do. That being said, even if I wasn't focused on building a career, I still wouldn't feel guilty. I'm twenty-three years old with my whole life ahead of me. There is no rush to build a career, there is no timeline on life that we have to follow. If you decide you want to travel for thirty years while living off enough money just to survive and then at fifty years old, you decide you want to start building your career, then there's absolutely nothing wrong with that.

My favourite aspect of becoming a digital nomad: no university degree needed! There are no previous skills or qualifications required for the majority of roles. A lot of roles might just require a short course to be completed to develop your skills. It really is possible for everyone.

Here are the different things I've done for work while travelling:

■ **e-Commerce:** The selling of products through online services. This was something I learned through an online company, who have a number of different courses to make money online and this was the path I chose to take. Their course content and experienced e-Commerce mentor guided me through each step. Starting from showing me the platforms to use, to support with finding best-selling products and helping me hire a virtual assistant to take the workload away from me. This path required a high amount of effort and dedication for the first three months or so, then after that I had systems in place and virtual assistants that carried the majority of my workload.

■ **Online English Teaching:** This can be done with or without a university degree. You will need to complete an online TEFL (Teaching English as a Foreign Language) course, which you usually get six months to complete. You can complete the course in your own time, however if you would like to finish it as soon as possible, you can most likely complete it within a few weeks. The course includes both question box assessments and written assignments.

Once you have your TEFL qualification, you can start applying for teaching jobs. There are certain companies that require a university degree, but there are many that will only require a TEFL certificate. Depending on which company you choose, there are different options to what age ranges you teach. For me, I taught children in China aged four to fourteen. It may also be useful to know that some companies will do the lesson planning for you, while others will require you to plan your own lessons. The company website will have all this information for you to read through before you apply for the job.

English teaching was a great online job to have—I chose my own schedule; it was fun and very rewarding.

◙ **Kindle Direct Publishing (KDP):** KDP is a self-publishing platform on Amazon. You are able to publish e-books, paperbacks and hardcover books for free. The best thing is that you don't need to be a writer to do this. So far, I have self-published e-book products on KDP and I'll soon be publishing this book in a paperback form using the same platform.

There are many different styles of books you can publish. If you don't want to write a lot, low-content books may be an option for you. These could have the same design on each page, with the same questions repeated for people to answer themselves on blank lines below. Questions like "What am I grateful for today?" and "What is one task I want to complete today?" for example, are great for low content book ideas.

You could create stories, guides, diaries, journals. The best thing is that there are no start-up costs. You can h pay for advertisements, which will increase your sale percentage.

◙ **Travel Group Leader:** While travelling, I have also worked with the tour company, as a group leader. I have shown different groups of travellers around Thailand. From the temples in Bangkok to floating bungalows in a national park, experiencing an overnight sleeper train, full moon parties, boat trips, elephant sanctuaries and sleeping overnight in the Chiang Mai jungle. Sounds fun?

This was something I wanted to do to challenge myself. It was far out of my comfort zone to be speaking in front of large groups of people, who were relying on me to keep them safe and show them the best time of their lives. I learned a lot, gained a lot of confidence, had so much fun and met the most amazing people.

There are many travel companies with career opportunities. This may be a good option for you if you'd like to travel with a set income each month.

When I first went travelling alone, I actually went with this same company for one of my trips. This was the trip that sparked my love for travel, and technically the trip that changed my life. It was extremely rewarding to give other people the same life-changing experience I once had myself.

Here are the profitable and successful career paths I've seen other travellers doing along the road:

- ◈ Virtual Assistant Services
- ◈ Online Coach (any subject you're skilled in)
- ◈ Customer Service Advisor
- ◈ Website Developer
- ◈ Amazon FBA
- ◈ Social Media Management
- ◈ Content Creator
- ◈ Article/Blog Writing
- ◈ Search Engine Optimisation (SEO) Specialist
- ◈ Copywriter
- ◈ Logo Designer
- ◈ Graphic Designer
- ◈ App Developer
- ◈ Video Creator
- ◈ Programmer
- ◈ Affiliate Marketing
- ◈ Sell an online course for a subject you're skilled in (e.g. photography)

The options aren't limited to the above. If you have your own skill, see if you can find a way to turn it into a freelancing service or business, or you can apply for remote job roles on LinkedIn or regular job application sites. Working abroad doesn't just have to be a digital nomad role either, you could look into working a season in Ibiza or work in your profession in Australia for example.

When looking for online work, please be wary of the scams and digital nomad bullshitters out there. Although there are a lot of legit online companies, there are still many scammers around and we just need to be aware and trust our guts. If someone is *promising* you that you can make £10K a month, within your first month, by joining their online course, it's probably a scam. No online business model can guarantee you any specific salary. The amount of money you make will depend on the amount of work you put in and it will slowly build up over time. You will probably be able to tell if a company is trustworthy or not—if it looks too good to be true, it might just as well be.

◼ **Work environments**: I've found that although you have to be comfortable with occasionally moving around and adapting to new environments, I work best when I can make a routine and stick to it. You may need to try out working in different places to find where and how you work the best. You might find that being surrounded by other people in a café will motivate you to work harder, a co-working space might just be the quiet spot you need, or a sun lounger on the beach might be your new favourite office chair.

Pay attention to where you work the best because being a digital nomad doesn't have to mean changing environments every other day if you find having a set routine for a certain amount of time works best for you. Some people strive when being on the go and working in a different area every day, others prefer to stick to one place for a while and occasionally change up their environment when they feel like it.

To take the first step, I suggest you put all of your focus on developing your skills in the area you've chosen to work in. You should then work out your budget and plan your finances to figure out how you can make it work. However, don't spend *too* much time developing skills and working out your finances.

Every professional started from somewhere, but they didn't wait long before they made a start. You will learn along the way by taking action, not by *planning* to take action. Take the leap and have some faith in yourself. Turn your travel bucket list into your to-do list.

Hopefully, this chapter has settled your money worries or has given you some ideas on how to make it work. If not, you could try speaking to other people you know who have travelled, listening to travel podcasts or reading travel blogs to find out how they made it work. Hopefully, someone out there can help you build up the courage to make it happen.

I ONCE SPOKE TO A SEVEN-YEAR-OLD GIRL FROM CHINA ABOUT different jobs. I went through different types of jobs and asked, "Do you want to be a nurse? A dancer? A farmer?"

After every job, she told me that she didn't have the time to do that job, so I asked her what she did want to be when she grew up.

She said, "I just want to be me because being me makes me happy."

She said that being herself made her happy because she wasn't that busy. When I reminded her that she'd just said she didn't have the time, she said that she didn't have the time to do things that didn't make her happy.

> *So if you really have no idea what you want to do, you can always just be yourself like this girl. I think one day she might need to combine 'being herself' with making some money, but this conversation I had with her made me think deeply about what made me happy. I know that whatever career path I end up on in life, it will have to bring me purpose.*
>
> *When I was a child and someone asked me what I wanted to be when I grew up, I said that I wanted to be a princess. When I dig deep to look into why I wanted to be a princess, it was because I valued time and freedom. I wanted to live a lifestyle where I didn't have to schedule my day around someone else's instructions. Those are still my greatest values to this day and although I'm now aware that my dream of becoming a real-life princess will most likely not come true, I know I can travel and work at the same time, which still provides me with the freedom I always desired.*

That's enough about being a princess, but remember, if you run out of money, there is nothing to stop you from going back home and getting another job. Just make sure you always have enough money for a flight home.

You need to find your **Why**. Why do you truly want this? Asking yourself this question should help you with saving money because when it gets difficult, you will always have your reason why in your mind that keeps you going.

> "Security is mostly superstition. It does not exist in nature, nor do the children of men as a whole experience it. Avoiding danger is no safer in the long run than outright exposure. Life is either a daring adventure, or nothing."
>
> Helen Keller—Educator and author.

When we see success as something we can design ourselves, we stop comparing our lives to others.

@elizacroft_

CREATING YOUR BUCKET LIST

What experiences do you want to have in the next phase of your life?

I hope you're all feeling inspired and have thought about some places you'd love to visit. However, if you haven't already got lots of destinations in mind, here is a list of things I've done and places I've been to, as well as my own bucket list that I hope to tick off in the near future. Hopefully, this might give you a few more ideas about which parts of the world you want to visit.

PLACES I'VE BEEN TO & THINGS I'VE DONE

- ◈ Saw the Niagara Falls in Canada
- ◈ Drove a campervan around Europe
- ◈ Swam with Manta Rays
- ◈ Swam with turtles
- ◈ Visited New York City
- ◈ Did an overnight cruise on Ha Long Bay in Vietnam
- ◈ Beach hopped in Australia
- ◈ Took rickshaw and tuk-tuk rides in Asia
- ◈ Attended a Balinese ceremony
- ◈ Skied in Finland

- ◈ Climbed the Eiffel Tower in Paris
- ◈ Island hopped in the Philippines
- ◈ Canyoneered in the Philippines
- ◈ Swam with whale sharks
- ◈ Visited an elephant sanctuary
- ◈ Slept overnight in the jungle

MY BUCKET LIST

- ◈ Skydiving
- ◈ Swim with pigs in the Bahamas
- ◈ Drive Route 66 in Scotland
- ◈ Experience a safari in South Africa
- ◈ Visit local villages in Africa
- ◈ Visit the Great Wall of China
- ◈ Visit the pyramids in Egypt
- ◈ Visit the Taj Mahal, India
- ◈ Take a hot air balloon in Cappadocia
- ◈ Volunteer in local villages and schools
- ◈ Trek to gorillas in Uganda
- ◈ Visit Costa Rica
- ◈ Visit Sri Lanka
- ◈ Visit Angkor Wat, Cambodia
- ◈ Visit Mexico
- ◈ Visit Brazil
- ◈ Visit Japan

CREATE YOUR BUCKET LIST

◈ . . . .
◈ . . . .
◈ . . . .
◈ . . . .
◈ . . . .
◈ . . . .
◈ . . . .
◈ . . . .
◈ . . . .
◈ . . . .
◈ . . . .
◈ . . . .
◈ . . . .
◈ . . . .
◈ . . . .
◈ . . . .
◈ . . . .
◈ . . . .
◈ . . . .
◈ . . . .
◈ . . . .
◈ . . . .
◈ . . . .

Although you may not be in a position to tick off everything on your bucket list, you can make a start on the places that are attainable at this point in your life.

As you look at where you want to go, think about the reasoning behind wanting to do these things: Personal growth? Learn about other cultures? See more of the world?

BUDGET TRAVEL

To travel as cheaply as possible, it's a sensible idea to choose the best budget destinations for first-time solo travellers, rather than choosing to travel somewhere you would most likely spend your monthly budget in a week. Below are listed some of the most well-known places for budget travel, as well as overlooked budget destinations.

Let's start with my obvious favourite place—Bali, Indonesia.

Bali and its surrounding islands are a perfect destination for backpackers on a budget. When I first arrived in Bali, I unintentionally splashed out on eating at the Instagramable cafés and restaurants which was costing me around the same price I'd pay in the U.K. When the balance in my bank account started to drop, I decided to switch my eating habits and eat at local restaurants and at places that had a promotional offer. This could have saved me a lot of money when I first arrived there.

In Bali, it's possible to get a meal for £1.80 at a local restaurant and there are a lot of accommodations for less than £10 a night. Bali is a backpacker's dream. If you'd like more information on Bali, I have a Bali Guide available on Amazon, called '21 Days Bali Adventure Guide & Itinerary'. It's extremely affordable and it includes a ready-made itinerary, restaurant and accommodation recommendations, useful contact numbers for transport and activity companies, apps to download and everything I wish I'd known before I travelled to Bali.

The Philippines can be another great destination for budget travellers, *if you plan thoroughly in advance.* The food is cheap, except in Western restaurants. If you eat the local food, it's a lot cheaper and there are some great local dishes in the Philippines. Accommodation is also cheap. You can stay in hostels for £7 to £10 per night. I also stayed in a few budget hotels where rooms ranged from £11 to £25 per night.

However, as I discussed earlier on in the book, if you want to travel to the Philippines on a budget, you need to book internal flights in advance. The Philippines is made up of four thousand islands so you will need to catch a flight or ferry to each place, which will work out expensive if you book the internal transport last minute.

If you're a budget traveller, you must visit Thailand. It's a popular destination for first-time solo travellers and you can live on a small budget. Thai food is amazing and local dishes range from £1 to £5.

Using my Booking.com loyalty discounts, I paid £5 per night at my accommodation when I first arrived. Thailand is cheaper inland and in the Chang Mai region. Transport to each different area in Thailand is extremely affordable, with most ferries costing around £5 and flights from as low as £25. I'm not sure why it took me so long to visit Thailand, but now I'm here, I can see why everyone visits and there's a reason the country is referred to as 'The Land of Smiles'.

Other Asian countries such as Vietnam, Cambodia, Sri Lanka and Laos are all popular destinations for budget travellers. Vietnam is one of the cheapest Asian countries and is full of beautiful scenery and attractions. If you want to travel on a budget and you like living simply, exploring beautiful islands and enjoying every moment of life, then Asia is the place for you.

Asia also has some great cities to explore, including Kuala Lumpur, Bangkok and Singapore. To put the prices in Malaysia into context, a Nando's cost me £5.50, whereas in the U.K I used to pay £14!

Singapore is definitely not a place I'll be adding as a budget destination. A pint of beer is £10+. My friends recently visited Singapore and paid £400 for a one-night stay in one of the city's fanciest hotels. It had a rooftop pool overlooking the city, but they were only allotted a one-hour time slot. If you're a budget traveller, stick to the hostels!

In my opinion, Turkey is very underrated for travellers. On a backpacker budget, you can live off under £30 a day. Turkey has beautiful beaches and lots of great tourist attractions. I personally loved Turkey as it reminded me of Asia, with a bit more expense added. Although some countries are considered 'cheap', I find it difficult to view anywhere as a budget destination after travelling to South East Asia. It's difficult to find anywhere with better prices.

Greece is considered expensive by a lot of people, but it's possible to travel on a budget if you stay in cheap accommodation and eat the local food. Island hopping is a popular way to get around Greece. Mexico can be cheap if you visit the right areas. Places like Playa Del Carmen and Chiapas State are considered to be some of the cheapest areas of Mexico.

From my own experience and from the experiences of friends who I've met while travelling, the cheapest backpacker budget destinations are South East Asia, the Indian Subcontinent and most of Central America.

Travelling can be done on several different budget styles. I've personally travelled on a 'social budget', where I've been out partying every other night. I've travelled on an activity budget, where I went on adventures and participated in new activities every day. I've travelled on a working budget where I've worked online while travelling. I've travelled on a savings budget where I didn't work at all and lived off savings and I've also travelled on an extremely tight budget where I ate bread and eggs every day for lunch and Nasi Goreng for dinner (Balinese dish, £0.65) to save me some money so that I could travel for longer (I don't recommend doing this).

Each experience was different, but my favourite has to be the time I travelled on an activity/adventure budget. This time in my life brought me so much freedom, happiness and adrenaline.

Although I would never want to be in a position again where I'm limiting my food intake to save some pennies, I'm grateful to have had that experience as it put me in a position where I was forced to figure out another way of making money. This 'tight budget' period didn't last long for me, it was a matter of weeks before I realised that not being able to afford a decent meal was manifesting into my reality. I'm a strong believer in the power of manifestation and if you constantly say to yourself, "I can't afford it," then you will never be able to afford it.

As soon as I stopped stressing, overthinking my money situation and telling myself that I couldn't afford to eat meals that I wanted to eat, things started to change. Remote work came my way and other opportunities to make money arrived on my doorstep.

Now I'm not saying eat at fancy restaurants every day in the hope that you might be able to afford to do that, but pay attention to the things you're telling yourself and the actions you're taking, because the things that get delivered to you in life always align with your thoughts and actions. I started eating the food I enjoyed again, going out with my friends more often and I started to believe that money would come my way whenever I needed it (and it usually does).

I still lived on a tight budget. I wouldn't eat out for every meal and I wouldn't buy as much alcohol, if any, when I went on a night out. But I didn't live a life according to my thoughts of 'I can't afford that', so that these thoughts would not then become a reality. You will overcome any obstacle thrown at you. For every problem, there is a solution.

Unfortunately the first time I travelled I didn't pay attention to what I spent. Had I known that I'd write a book about travel a few years later, I would definitely have calculated every penny that came out of my pocket. After I came home, I did calculate a rough estimate of my spending, but I couldn't guarantee that it was anywhere near accurate.

Below is a list of what I spent on the different budget styles I've travelled on:

◈ Travel to Bali, Australia and Vietnam for one month without tight budgeting and partying most nights. This included an organised tour group in Bali (around £800), our one-way flights (U.K. – Bali – Australia – Vietnam – U.K), accommodation, food and lifestyle/activity spending. In total, I spent around £4000. This can be done *a lot* cheaper if you were to budget appropriately.

◈ Activity budget whereby I spent most days doing activities, going on adventures, day trips and trying new sports classes. In six weeks, the activities in Bali cost me £155, accommodation cost £560 for single occupancy (I didn't stay in hostels, which could have made it cheaper), £60 for gyms and fitness classes and around £200 for food. In total, this cost around £975. If I was to include flights in this price, it would total to an estimate of around £1675 for six weeks.

◈ Living abroad in Bali on an extremely tight budget— This is the time I limited my food, stopped eating out for every meal and limited my lifestyle activities. I spent around £100 on food (making sure every meal was under £5 and doing a weekly food shop that would cover my breakfast and lunch for the week). My villa rent cost me £280 per month (before I changed accommodation, which then lowered my costs to £150 per month) and to rent my moped cost £30 a month. I spent £45 to extend my visa each month, travel insurance cost me £30 and mobile phone data cost me £1.60 per month. Within this month, I didn't completely stop doing activities and eating out, I probably did this around once a week. Living on a seriously tight budget cost me around £500 to £600 for one month.

As you can see, each budget style was in a similar time scale of four to six weeks. However, the expenses were dramatically different. Travelling solo can work out to be extremely cheap but can also be quite expensive. This all depends on whether you pay attention to what you're spending, which accommodation type you stay in, how often you party, what kind of lifestyle you want to live and how last-minute you are with booking your trip. Apart from Australia, my budget styles are all from South East Asia, which is probably the cheapest place to travel to. Your monthly costs will depend on which country you choose to travel to. Research your chosen destination to see how much you need to have saved for the period you want to visit.

Whichever budget style you choose, you should ◨ implement a budget strategy that won't put your future under unnecessary financial stress.

LIVING ABROAD

My life-changing idea came to me while I was sitting at my desk in my hospital office job. This was the moment I decided I was going to live in Bali, Indonesia. I told myself twelve months, at least. I didn't think too much about it, this felt like the right gut decision. The same day, I went home and broke the news to my boyfriend and six months later I had quit my job, broke up with my boyfriend, packed my bags and left the U.K.

At the time this idea of living abroad came to me, I was craving travel and a new adventure. When I was thinking of which country to live in, I thought of a place where I'd had some of the best experiences, a place with kind people, somewhere with a good lifestyle and somewhere that could challenge me. I felt called to Indonesia, more than to any other country.

But as the pandemic was ongoing, it was impossible to do the travelling I wanted to do. I decided that sticking to one country for now would be better than no travel at all. I followed a lot of women on Instagram that had set up their lives in Indonesia. They inspired me to make the move and showed me that it was possible.

For two reasons, the process was quite simple. First, I had few responsibilities at home. I had no house to sell, no job that I was desperate to keep and I was twenty-two years old. The second reason was that the moving process to Indonesia is simple as long as you have the correct visa. (Visa regulations are constantly changing. For updated information on Bali visas, I would recommend checking out a company called *Bali Solve* who can be found on Google or Instagram).

I loved living in Bali. Although it was challenging at times, it was a real eye-opener for me. Arriving there solo allowed me to take the time as a period of reflection, learn a little more about myself and what path I wanted to head towards, as well as having the opportunity to explore the beautiful island I got to call home and meet the amazing people I've been so lucky to cross paths with. I fell in love with my life there, every single moment, even the struggles I faced, because the struggles make us stronger. They guide us onto the right path, and encourage us to push even harder than before.

My original plan wasn't to live abroad. I merely wanted to travel and explore lots of different countries. I was on a mission to experience as much of the world as possible. I suppose living abroad has been as close to settling down as I'll get any time soon. Although I can't really call it 'settling down' since I moved into four different homes while living in Asia.

For the first few months of living abroad, I travelled around Bali to see as much of it as possible before I decided to move to one specific area to settle and form some kind of routine. Around three months into the 'routine life', I started craving travel again. I couldn't keep still. Bali was my home away from home and I think I will always be drawn back here no matter where I go in the world. Even though I knew I was in a place where I could travel wherever and whenever I wanted to, I still knew that I needed to respect my sense of adventure and freedom, which meant that I needed to visit other places to feel inspired and creative again. No matter where I was, if

I stayed in the same place for too long, I started to feel stuck and my creativity and energy levels decreased. I was lucky enough to live on a beautiful island where I could take myself away for the weekend if I found myself craving adventure.

To live abroad, you need to ensure you have the correct visa by speaking with a visa agency. You need to find out if you're eligible to work and which visa you will need to do so. Don't forget about the little things such as selling your car, cancelling your insurances, cancelling your utility accounts, decluttering your house and looking into tax obligations. If you are planning to live in one place as opposed to travelling around, take as much with you as possible, rather than paying expensive postage and tax fees to get items shipped out afterwards, (the exception of packing light comes to the fore if you're moving there to live).

You will most likely need to open a bank account in your destination country and consider whether you want to close the bank account in your home country or speak to your bank to see if they'll allow you to keep it open. See if you can find a bank that (almost) rules out transaction fees. If you're on a working visa and are working under a company, your employer may be able to help with this.

To find housing, I'd personally recommend only committing to a place once you've viewed it in person. In Indonesia for example, there are a lot of villas online with images that look nothing like they do in reality. You don't want to commit to twelve months in a villa before you've seen it with your own eyes and checked out the surrounding area. From my own experience in Indonesia, there are plenty of properties available, so there is no rush to find housing before you arrive. You can spend a week or so in a hotel while you have a look around. It's a good idea to connect with travellers who have already experienced moving to your chosen country. You can most likely find Facebook groups for people who have moved to that specific country.

You should also research transportation options before you move abroad. Look into which type of transport is most popular and most efficient to get around your destination country. Unfortunately, my ability to drive a car was of no use at all to me in Indonesia and I had to learn a completely new skill of driving a moped (yes, I consider this a skill).

If you are driving abroad, you will need to get an international driver's license from your home country before you arrive. These are usually cheaper to get at home than it is to apply for a new license abroad.

You will also need to consider how you will support yourself financially when living abroad, whether this means finding employment or one of the options I discussed in the 'I Can't Afford It' chapter. Sitting down to create a budget plan may seem like a lot of effort and something that you might find yourself procrastinating with, but it's an extremely useful tool to have that can decrease your money worries during your move. Aside from working, I have met a lot of people during my travels who are completing their university degrees online while travelling or living abroad. This could be an option if your degree allows you to study remotely.

My main issue with moving abroad was deciding to change phone numbers and completely discard my U.K. number. I hadn't thought it through enough. My U.K. number was connected to every single account I owned. Evidently, I had forgotten my passwords to pretty much all of my accounts and the only way back into them was to get a verification code sent to my U.K. number, which didn't exist anymore. I spent weeks on the phone with customer service advisors trying to gain access to my email accounts and different accounts where I held my money. So if you're going to change phone numbers, please make sure you update the verification number on all of your accounts first, unless you want to willingly increase your stress levels.

Some may say (including myself) that my experience of moving abroad was much smoother for me than for someone with more responsibilities or for someone moving to a country with stricter regulations.

To decide which country you'd like to live in, a few things you need to consider are:

◈ Cost of living
◈ Accessibility—is it possible to live there long term? Consider transport routes and how easy it is to travel in and out of the country if needed.
◈ Safety
◈ Work—how easy is it to find work? Is the job market wide enough?
◈ Climate
◈ Do you feel confident living there because you've visited before? Or are you wanting to challenge yourself to somewhere completely new?

Moving abroad can either go smoothly or be challenging, but either way, you will need to prepare yourself for the change that comes with it.

> *"Certainly, travel is more than the seeing of sights; it is a change that goes on, deep and permanent, in the ideas of living."*
>
> Mary Ritter Beard—Historian

The struggles make us stronger. They guide us onto the right path, and encourage us to push even harder than before.

@elizacroft_

BEFORE YOU GO CHECKLIST

Don't worry, you won't need to read back through the whole book again to check you've done everything before you set off on your travels. I got you. Here is a list of tasks you'll need to complete before you travel. I've left some space at the end for you to add any other important tasks.

◈ Check your passport has more than six months validity until its expiry date (and that it's not going to expire while you're travelling)

◈ Purchase travel insurance (if travelling long-term, check your chosen insurance company covers long periods)

◈ Check if you need a visa for the country you're visiting, and which type you may need. For example, if you plan on working abroad, you will most likely need a different visa than if you were travelling as a tourist

◈ Exchange money—give yourself some time for this as the money may have to be ordered into the bank

◈ Check travel restrictions and entry requirements—PCR tests, fill out pertinent forms, book quarantine if necessary

◈ Stock up on medications & other health products

◈ Research recommended vaccinations or ask your GP

◈ Attend any check-up appointments you may need—dentist, doctor, optician

◈ Make copies of all documents

◈ Apply for an international driver's licence (if needed)—these are around £5 from the post office so it's worth getting one, even if you're not sure whether you'll be driving abroad

◈ Check in online for your flight. Sometimes the airline will allow you to do this at the airport

◈ Download all recommended travel apps

◈ Join Facebook groups for destinations you plan to visit

Create your own checklist here:

◈ . . . .
◈ . . . .
◈ . . . .
◈ . . . .
◈ . . . .
◈ . . . .
◈ . . . .
◈ . . . .
◈ . . . .
◈ . . . .
◈ . . . .
◈ . . . .
◈ . . . .
◈ . . . .
◈ . . . .
◈ . . . .
◈ . . . .
◈ . . . .
◈ . . . .
◈ . . . .
◈ . . . .
◈ . . . .
◈ . . . .
◈ . . . .
◈ . . . .
◈ . . . .
◈ . . . .
◈ . . . .
◈ . . . .
◈ . . . .

THE SCHOOL OF TRAVEL

LESSONS GIFTED

You could say this chapter is me throwing out some life lessons. Am I too young to be providing life lessons? Possibly. Let's change it to the lessons that travel has gifted me. Travel is an opportunity for lifelong learning. It is a transformative experience that challenges stereotypes and opens you to a whole new world of living styles and cultural values.

Travelling solo has been my greatest education. It has taught me considerably more about life than traditional education has. There are many more ways to live than the way we're taught in school. The world is a classroom, not the one you sit down in for hours listening to lectures and clock-watching for the lesson duration. The world is a classroom where subjects are taught through experience, adventure, successes, failures, changes, challenges, twists and turns and bumps and bruises. Once you've been to a school like that, you'll never want the lesson to end. You'll want every day to be a school day. The world is a true education platform.

I never wanted to learn in school, I found learning boring. It was like a chore. As soon as I could leave the education system, I did. Don't get me wrong, I *loved* school, but this was because of the group of friends I had. We made each day a fun day. It was the learning itself that I just couldn't get myself to enjoy. What I didn't realise was that I was learning the wrong subjects, in the wrong way. I wanted to learn about life, how other cultures live and what there is to discover. But rather than learning about this through books and lectures, I wanted to learn about these subjects by seeing things with my own eyes. Experience is what makes information stick in my mind, experience is the most rewarding type of education we can be given.

Travelling isn't for everyone, but if it's for you then you'll know. My brother, George, would quite happily go on a two-week holiday with his mates for a piss-up instead of going travelling. It just doesn't appeal to him. However, he does enjoy adventurous holidays like skiing trips with his friends, which are amazing experiences. But when I ask him about travelling, he just isn't that interested and that's fine. He once came to visit me in Bali. I travelled around the entire island with him in the hope that it would make him love travel as much as I did. But as much as he loved the experience, he was very happy when it was time to go home, get back to work and have a night out with his friends.

You can't make anyone want to come travelling with you. You have to accept that some people are not interested and not everyone loves it the same way we do.

When you return home, all you will want to do is tell everyone about the life-changing experiences you just had. Not many people will want to listen. It's a little like when my dad talks to me about football—I don't understand it, therefore I don't listen. Don't take it to heart as I did when I returned from my first solo trip. You will find people who share the same love for travel as you do.

TRAVEL HAS STRETCHED MY MIND WITH NEW EXPERIENCES.
I've noticed how little other people have compared to us, as
Westerners. I once met a group of people while travelling in
the Philippines. We decided to rent mopeds and drive forty-five
minutes to a beach, which the locals warned us not to go to as
it was a terrible drive. We decided to take on the challenge, but
they weren't wrong about it being a difficult drive. On the first
day that we attempted the drive, it started raining as soon as we
arrived at the beach so we stopped off in a local village where a
lady gave us some drinks and we watched the children playing
games in the rain. The rain didn't stop, so we decided to head
back and I'm surprised we didn't end up over the side of a cliff.
The whole drive back was on rocky, clay-like roads. We were
sliding instead of driving, with a few near-miss falls on the way.

However, for some unusual reason, we all decided we
wanted to go back the next day when the sun was out. I'm so
glad we did. It was probably the best day I've ever had while
travelling. We had a bumpy drive there, but when we arrived
at the beach, the sun was shining and fifteen kids came run-
ning up to us, giving us hi-fives. As this beach was difficult to
get to and because of the pandemic, they hadn't seen so many
tourists in years.

They were running into the sea doing front flips. They were
falling on their heads and getting straight back up to do another
flip. We played games on the beach with them all day; tag,
football, volleyball and gymnastics. They didn't stop laughing
and neither did we. I hadn't played games for as long as that
since I was a child myself.

The kids didn't have any phones or iPads. They had just
one flat volleyball between them. They never watched videos on
phones and they were crying with laughter when we showed them
the clips we had shot of them playing. This day was extremely

wholesome and I came away with a heart full of gratitude for being able to experience this with the happiest Filipino children and amazing friends I'd met while solo travelling. It made me think back to the children at home who were upset if they didn't have the latest iPhone. At some point in our childhoods, the majority of us have probably been upset over not having something that is considered a luxury.

After this day, I noticed a change in my thoughts and I was more aware of any slight complaints I made over minor problems. The hotel I was staying in had a bad signal and I found myself frustrated for the first day or so. After spending a day with these children, I went back to the same hotel and my Wi-Fi wasn't working, but this time I just accepted it and put my phone away. We don't need internet all of the time, it's a luxury. The same with many other things that we'd complain about if we were to be without them for a while. Seeing the kids so happy with so little, just enjoying their time playing in the village, is a memory and feeling I'll never forget.

As well as travel teaching you about the interesting cultures and mesmerising history of the places you visit, travel uniquely reveals things about yourself. Although I consider myself an introvert and I'm at peace with my own company, I've learnt that I hate being alone too. Yes, I need that time to myself when socialising gets a little too much, but I also notice that I start to feel lonely and homesick if I spend too much time by myself. I crave human connections and this is something that we all need, no matter how much we love spending time by ourselves.

Travelling solo has made me figure out how I like to spend my time. My sixteen to nineteen-year-old self, who used to party every weekend, as well as attend the odd 'Thursday

Club' and turn up to college hungover the next day, would be shocked if she knew that I didn't enjoy drinking alcohol and partying (that much) anymore.

I love to spend my time reading, journaling, exercising, creating, writing, exploring and trying new things. Boring? *Someone just pass her a drink.* But these are the things I've figured out I enjoy the most, none of which I knew I enjoyed before I travelled, before I became a little more self-aware and paid attention to the things that make me feel good. I never actually knew what I enjoyed, I thought I just enjoyed going out at the weekend, but these other things make me feel free, inspired and happy.

Some boundaries and limits of mine have surprisingly made an appearance too. I never even knew what having boundaries felt like.

If someone asked me to go shopping with them when I had to revise for an exam that day, I'd say, "Let's do it!"

If someone asked me to go to the gym when I felt like I was on my deathbed, I'd say, "I can't let you down!"

If someone asked me to go on a night out when I had work at 8 am the next morning, I'd say, "Hell yes, let's stay out until the club closes!"

When I first started travelling, I said yes to everyone and everything. I felt like I was obliged to make plans every single day so that I wouldn't block myself from any opportunity of making friends. I soon came to realise that even if you say no to the night out or cancel the lunch date because you just don't feel like going, your new friends will still want to hang out another day and they will probably appreciate you more for having boundaries. I used to make up excuses for not going out, but now I just tell people I don't feel like it. Having no boundaries is exhausting. If you don't have them, think of what you'd like them to be, I promise they'll make your life a lot easier.

When you travel, you will find out what your limits are and what type of traveller you are because everyone has personal preferences. You will learn what type of places you prefer to travel to. I prefer islands with beaches where the people live with simplicity and at a slower pace than people in cities. Although I've always said I don't like cities, I've visited Kuala Lumpur a few times and that city changed my whole perspective. I loved it there and I couldn't count the number of times I said, "Wow."

New York was also one of those 'wow' cities for me. However, I know that once I've visited a city, I'm not likely to go back unless I need to, no matter how amazing it was. I prefer to spend my time on the beach in the sun.

You might not like sharing a room in hostels with strangers, you might not like staying in accommodation with outside bathrooms, you might like travelling at a faster or slower pace, you might like staying in areas with good nightlife or you may prefer to get up early to go sightseeing. Personally, squat toilets are something I struggle to use and I'm a little tired of sharing outside bathrooms with wildlife. I make exceptions with squat toilets when there are no other options.

YOU HAVE NO OTHER CHOICE IN THE PHILIPPINES. ONCE IT WAS a little worse than a squat toilet. In fact, there was no toilet at all. The shop owner laughed as she opened a door and told me to pee on the floor and they would clean it up afterwards. After an eight-hour island hopping boat tour and my body refusing to let me urinate in the sea, I was just happy they offered me their floor space and I didn't hesitate to lower my standards.

Travel might seem all glamorous when you see pictures of stunning beaches, but there are aspects of it that aren't as glam and you'll learn whether you're happy to accommodate those or whether this is where your limits are.

Travel taught me that 'home' is wherever you are. A home is a place where you feel comfortable and at ease. You will always find this by doing inner work. It has taught me to have faith in myself and that I really am capable of achieving anything I put my mind to. I've met people who have made unbelievable and inspiring achievements. These people are just ordinary people who are pursuing the things that excite them. They go for every opportunity that's placed in front of them. For me, being surrounded by people like this has enhanced my progression in my career and my confidence. It has helped me overcome my fears a lot faster than I would have progressed if I had worked alone or had been surrounded by people who didn't push me to do better.

You will start to attract people who are striving for similar goals to you, or people who have already done what it is that you're working towards. Use these people for support and inspiration. While writing this book, I met seven other people who are published authors, or are in the process of becoming one. I can't tell you how reassuring and encouraging it's been to have had these people alongside me in the process. You may feel alone when you first set off to travel, or try something new, but by doing so, you will always attract people who you need for support to show you that you're on the right track.

Being surrounded by people who are taking risks and pushing themselves to become 1% better every day, has also helped me not to care what other people think (I'm still working on this, but I'm getting there). If you're always worried about what other people think, you will slow down your progression in life and you will never end up pursuing the things you dream of. I have learnt how to express myself. I have complete faith in my abilities and I now love myself a lot more than I ever did before I travelled.

I've learnt that I'm awful at navigation. Even when I've been to a place before and think I know where I'm going, or even when I'm using Google Maps, my senses tell me to go a different way and I always end up adding an extra twenty minutes onto my journey. Today is a great example of my bad navigation skills. I'm currently writing this book in a co-working space with my friend. I arranged to meet her here at 9am and I arrived at 09:37 am (I live an eight-minute drive away). Don't ask.

I've discovered I enjoy a lot more activities than I thought I would. I never thought I'd enjoy quad biking, pole tricks, or driving a moped (after the many stressful times of almost driving into a cyclist, swerving to the opposite side of the road and being in a crash on a highway, alone, in the middle of nowhere). If you're not living in the country and a moped isn't absolutely necessary for you to get around, I *highly* recommend you stick to taxi mopeds or cars instead.

Trying lots of different activities while travelling has made me realise that adults need to play too. Fun and games aren't just for children. Adults need to express themselves, open up, release emotions and have fun. This is what travel offers.

I've also come to learn that self-care isn't just bubble baths and face masks. Self-care is setting your boundaries, saying no to the things you don't want to do without having to explain yourself to others, and saying yes to the things that bring you excitement.

Self-care is eating food that feels good for your mind and body.

It's taking good care of your body by exercising in a way that feels good for you.

Self-care can be breathing deeply when you feel overwhelmed.

It can be healing from traumas.

It can be asking for help before you really need it.

It can be fully accepting your emotions without guilt or judgement. Allow yourself to process these sensations you're feeling.

Self-care is doing the things that feel good for you, not the things other people recommend doing as self-care. That can feel good for them but it might not work for you.

First-world problems *are not* a big deal. Seeing how families live in different countries will open your eyes to how easy most of our day-to-day lives are.

We shouldn't complain about having to go to work, other people are desperate for a job.

We shouldn't complain that our phone or laptop is broken, other people have never even held one in their hands.

We shouldn't complain about having to wash the dishes, be grateful that you've just been able to eat a full meal that has made those dishes dirty.

We are far more privileged than any of us realise. I've learnt to value experiences over materialistic items.

Being rich in experience is the greatest form of wealth.

*Being rich
in experience
is the greatest
form of wealth.*

@elizacroft_

Travel has taught me that although we all live very different lives, we are all human and very much alike. You will make friends with people from all over the world, with those who are local and those who are travelling from different countries. You will make friends with those who you wouldn't see yourself being friends with in your hometown. Travel brings different people together who end up having more similarities than you would have first imagined.

I've learnt what's important to me and who's important to have in my life. I appreciate and value my friends and family more than ever.

People come into your life because they're there to teach you something, whether that be good or bad. Travel will make you realise who the people are that no longer bring value into your life. You will drift away from these people as they aren't meant to be in the next chapter of your life.

You will build connections with new people, who are present in your life to teach you something new and to push you into becoming a better version of yourself. As well as important people, you will also realise what's important to have in your life. You might decide that having the Rolls Royce you've always dreamt of isn't that important to you anymore, or you might discover that a Rolls Royce is now at the top of your vision board. You might decide that you value spending time with loved ones more than making money, or that you're extra driven to make the money to then be able to spend even more time with loved ones.

To me, the most important lesson that travel has taught me is that other people always need it more than I do. I've learnt to always give anything I can to those in need. Once you've given it away, you will notice that you didn't need that money, after all, you survived without it. You will realise that giving away your precious time to volunteer with a charity or to help your grandparents do the weekly food shop, does fit into your busy schedule when you make the time for it. Giving to others also gives you an unforgettable feeling which may feel even better for the person on the receiving end.

So, I'm not saying that we don't need traditional education, because of course we need to learn certain subjects to get by in life, or to learn specific subjects if we want to pursue a career in that field. But if I had to choose over traditional school or the school of travel, you can guess which one I'd be leaping towards.

WHY GO SOLO?

But how can solo travel be better than travelling with your friends? Doesn't it just get lonely?

I personally find it a lot easier to meet new people when I travel alone as opposed to when I travel with a friend or partner. Solo travel does not stop you from travelling with others. Solo travel is just another style of travel, which can be for as long or as little as you like.

When I went to Bali for the second time, I travelled for ten weeks with my sister Harriet. I noticed that because there were two of us, people wouldn't approach as much as if I'd been by myself, because they can see you've already got company and they don't think you're open to meeting more people. However, when I'm on my own, people will come up to me to make conversation because they can see I'm travelling solo. I also found that when I was with Harriet, I didn't make much of an effort to meet new people because I was already comfortable. When I travel solo, I make a conscious effort to speak to new people because number one, I love getting inspired by new people and number two, I actually want to make friends and not be alone for my whole trip.

Travelling with my sister was one of the best experiences I've ever had. We had both dreamed of travelling together since we were younger and we always said that as soon as she turned 18, we would go, so we did! I will forever cherish those memories we created together. We had some crazy adventures from sliding down waterfalls to attending Balinese ceremonies, to swimming with dolphins and manta rays.

As much as I'm immensely grateful for those memories, travelling solo has made me grow an incredible amount more than travelling with someone else did. It's pushed me out of my comfort zone and made me face my fears. I've built connections with people from all over the world and become more self-aware, educated and completely inspired by the people I've met and the places I've visited. I now make bold decisions, I'm more confident in myself and my abilities, and my vision of what I can achieve and who I can be has increased by an excessive amount.

I can physically and mentally feel the positive impact travelling solo has had on me, but it was only when my family came to visit me when I lived in Indonesia, that I truly became aware of how much it had changed me. They made comments on my appearance, confidence, independence and happiness. In my mum's words, "Never would I have thought that the quiet, shy, little girl would have turned out like this and created a life like this for herself." Now I'm not saying this to brag (although I am pretty proud of myself), but it was at this moment I realised how much I'd grown, how many surreal experiences I'd had and how **booking my first ever solo trip was the move that changed my life.**

I recently looked at the statistics for Google searches on female solo travel and the statistics for online bookings made by female solo travellers. They show that the community of women travelling solo is increasing year after year. The solo travel bookings have particularly increased post-pandemic. I always ask young women travelling solo why they do it. The overwhelming reasons are:

◈ Wanting to meet new people
◈ Wanting to do what they want, when they want
◈ Having different interests from their friends
◈ Partners not wanting to travel as much as they do
◈ Personal growth
◈ The feeling of freedom and independence
◈ To gain confidence
◈ To challenge themselves
◈ Not wanting to wait around for others.

More and more females heading off on solo trips is changing the perception of and breaking down the barriers to female solo travel. A lot of people seem to think that if you travel alone, you're not loved or not worthy because nobody wants to come with you. But other people may not have the same desire to travel as you have, so they will come up with any excuse not to go with you. The truth is, you don't need to feel valued by others if you value yourself. You can become whole on your own, which will give you the confidence to travel alone, while still feeling worthy of the love from others.

Travel didn't make me happy, being in beautiful environments and experiencing amazing things didn't make me happy. They played a part, but what made me truly happy was the work I did, and the work I'm still doing now, on my inner self. I taught myself to be happy wherever I was, whatever I was doing.

And while travel itself didn't make me happy, the people I met who inspired me, taught me that this work needed to be done. I always rejected the thought of doing any work on myself, because I thought I was happy enough. This rejection was down to my lack of self-awareness and the changes I now see within myself show that the work *did* need to be done. As soon as I kept consistent with this work, I became happier, that's when I started to love myself. I accepted that I didn't need anyone else or any external validation to make me happy.

I've spoken to a lot of people who think that going travelling will solve all their problems and make them happier. Even if you're lying on a beach in paradise, the problems that are inside of you will not be resolved by changing locations. You need to dig deep and find out what's causing these problems, the limiting beliefs, the unhappiness, because when you learn to be truly happy *within* yourself, you can be happy *wherever* you are in the world.

If you don't know where to start, start with gratitude. At the end of each day, think of three things that you were grateful for. It will condition your mind into looking out for things to be grateful for throughout every day.

Pay attention to the comments you make about yourself and the things that you complain about. When you do this, you'll start to notice how many negative comments you're making, which in turn affects your mood. Staying consistent with these small changes can have a huge effect on your overall happiness.

Travelling solo has been a game-changer in how I see the world. It has reinforced my independence and made me more considerate and grateful. You start to put yourself out there, you will develop the bravery and courage that's required to try things unfamiliar to you.

Travelling solo will increase your problem-solving skills. You have nobody to lean on to make decisions for you, so you are forced to figure out a way to solve your problems your-self. Trust me when I say I was the worst decision-maker you would have ever met. Ask me what I want to eat—"It's up to you." Ask me whether I'd like a cup of tea—"I don't mind." But being in a position where you can't ask your friend or your partner for quick advice forces you to make decisions and solve problems that arise *all by yourself.*

Travelling solo also makes you more spontaneous and creative. You will say yes to more opportunities and more adventures. Being exposed to different types of people and a different environment has made my creativity increase dramatically. I always considered myself someone awful at thinking of new ideas. I would purposely avoid applying for jobs that would have 'decision making and ability to think of new ideas' written in their job requirements.

However, I now have new ideas flowing from me every day. So much so that I have a journal dedicated only to new ideas and a notes page full of thoughts and ideas on my phone. I schedule a set time each week to sit and write down any ideas that come to me within twenty minutes (you'll be surprised at how many ideas pop up if you start thinking and writing anything that comes to mind). Without travel, I would most likely still be avoiding creative job opportunities, running away from any sort of 'group work idea activity'. and I would still be giving myself the identity of 'an uncreative person who can never think of her own ideas.'

When you travel solo, you're in charge of your sched-ule, you don't have anyone else to please and you don't have to justify your decisions to anyone apart from yourself. You can travel and adventure as much as you want or take as much relaxation time as you need, it's completely your own choice. I remember being at home, I would plan my schedule for the day, hour-by-hour, but I would never end up sticking to it. Apart from the occasional procrastination, one of the main reasons for this was changing my schedule at the last minute to fit in with what other people wanted me to do, (*cough*, my sister asking me for a lift to her friends' house). I was more than happy to do things for other people, but one of my boundaries should have been for them to ask me the day before so that I can plan my day around it. The point I'm getting at is, that when you travel solo, you don't have to add other people into your schedule, it's nice to have a break from people-pleasing and focus on yourself.

Travel is a huge opportunity for self-reflection and development when you indulge in spending time alone. You're able to sit with yourself and your thoughts. This might sound scary to some, but once you get used to it, being comfortable with sitting with yourself is a beautiful thing and a strong attribute to have.

You become more self-aware and get to know your strengths and weaknesses. You become more independent and fearless, to the point where you feel completely comfortable walking into a restaurant and asking for a table for one, (there was once a time when I'd get extremely anxious even at the thought of sitting alone in a restaurant, but now I purposely treat myself to a date night alone). Solo travel isn't easy if you've never done it before, but the benefits it brings are so worth it.

Travelling solo is powerful and a huge fast track to self-discovery.

> *"I wonder why it was that places are so much lovelier when one is alone."*
>
> Daphine Du Maurier—Writer

Travelling solo is powerful and a huge fast track to self-discovery.

@elizacroft_

ARE YOU EXPERIENCED?

B efore writing this book, I surveyed a range of female travellers with experience, as well as females that have the
desire to travel. Below is a summary of their responses. They
represent a good cross-section of views on the fears women
face before travelling and the transformed outlook they have
once they are experiencing travel.

QUESTIONS I ASKED
THOSE WHO HAVE NEVER TRAVELLED:

What is the thing holding you back from going travelling?

◼ **No money**—If travel is *really* something you want, you
either need to get disciplined at saving or find a way to earn
money while you travel. Have another read of my 'I Can't
Afford It' chapter where I discuss the options to save and earn
in detail.

◼ **No one to go with / Fear of being alone**—The majority
of people you'll meet on your travels will be travelling solo.
These people will most likely have the same worries that you
have and they'll also be looking to make friends. I discuss

the different ways I've made friends while travelling alone in the 'Turning Strangers Into Lifelong Friends' chapter. If you try out some of these options, you'll be guaranteed to make friends wherever you go! Once you've made that first friendship, the rest will start to flow more easily to you. But don't forget, not every friend you meet will end up being a solid friendship—meeting friends while travelling is similar to dating. You might go on one date with them and decide that the connection isn't quite there. Don't try to force friendships just so that you're not alone, just like you wouldn't force a relationship that wasn't going to work. The right friendships will come to you naturally without making too much effort.

◼ **Scared of flying**—If you don't think you can get on a flight, there are many countries you can visit by driving and taking a boat instead. When I travelled around Europe, I visited ten countries without catching a single flight.

◼ **Confidence in myself**—No matter what we do in life, whenever we try something new that's outside of our comfort zone, we will most likely question whether we're capable of achieving it or not. Try to step out of the fixed mindset that pushes you into believing you're not capable of achieving anything you're not familiar with. Step into the growth mindset where there's no limit to your potential and what you're capable of achieving. Whether you decide not to give it a try at all or try it and then decide it's not for you, you will still be in the same position; the only difference is that with the second option, you can say that you tried and gave it all you had. You might try it and notice that it's even better than you imagined it could be. You are capable of anything you put your mind to, no matter how daunting it may seem at first.

◼ **Being indecisive**—I didn't know anyone as indecisive as myself before I travelled. Travelling solo will force you to become a decisive person because you can't rely on other people to make your decisions. One thing I've come to understand recently is that only *you* know the answers. The only profound reason we ask others for their opinions is to feel approval and acceptance towards a decision we already know is the correct one for ourselves. It's *your* life, so why would you want someone else to make your decisions for you?

◼ **Having to do research**—If you don't like the idea of doing your own research, you can decide on the country you'd like to visit and then book a tour group, who will take away all the stress of you planning everything yourself. There are also lots of ready-made itineraries already out there for you to follow. Travel agents will be happy to help you plan your trip.

◼ **Pets at home that need caring for**—It's extremely upsetting to leave your pets behind for a while. You need to make sure they are left with someone whom you trust and someone you know they'll be comfortable with. Try asking family and friends first, but there are plenty of pet-sitter websites to find people in your area who will stay at your own house to look after your pet while you're away.

◼ **Not knowing what to do/how to get around/having no help**—No first-time traveller knows what they're doing. Even experienced travellers sometimes don't know what they're doing if they visit a country for the first time (including myself).

Not knowing what to do is all part of the experience. Every time you travel, you'll learn something new. You'll figure out 'better' ways to travel and you'll learn from the mistakes you made the last time. In terms of knowing how to get around, the more you ask questions and speak with locals or people who have been there a while, the more knowledge you will gain and the more contacts you'll have. Collecting as many contact numbers as you can in the area will be beneficial whenever you have a question—one of them will most likely know the answer. You'll be surprised at how many people will be willing to help you out. No matter what situation you get yourself in, there always seems to be someone around to help.

◼ **Not knowing where to start**—Take the first step. Ask yourself the questions I mentioned in the 'Getting Started' chapter and once you've decided on the places you're going to travel to, take the next step. Try not to look at it as one big job, just look at the first step, then the next, and the next and so on. Trying to plan everything at once will become overwhelming, which might result in you stopping the planning altogether.

◼ **I can't afford to travel as well as save for a house**—This comes down to your values. What do you value more: security and settling down, or adventure and experience? Neither of these answers are right or wrong, everyone has their preferences. If you want both, you could also set up two separate savings accounts which will enable you to save for both, it might just take a little longer to save for your house if you're also putting money elsewhere. But if you really value travel then this should be the way to go.

◼ **Getting leave from work**—This is another point I discussed in the 'I Can't Afford It' chapter. Have you asked your employer? You will never know whether your employer will grant you leave if you don't ask. If you can't get leave from work, you need to decide whether you value your position in your workplace more than experiencing travel. New opportunities will always arise. Sometimes the things that scare you the most are the things that will make you grow. During my time travelling, I've met people who have straight up quit their jobs to travel. I've also met people who have been granted a few months unpaid leave. And I've met people who have quit their corporate job and have found remote work so they can still earn money while travelling. I've also met people who are completing their university degrees online. There are different options, have a think of which one might be the best for you.

◾ **Worried it won't be the same after the Pandemic**—This can be viewed as a good thing or a bad thing. It's sad to see how many countries changed during the pandemic. Many businesses have closed and the usual tourist places emptied out. But more and more countries are rising from the ashes, tourists are starting to travel again and a lot of places are returning to something similar to how they used to be. And while travel is starting to start up again, there still aren't as many tourists as there used to be. Places aren't overcrowded anymore and you don't have to queue up for thirty minutes just to see a tourist attraction. With places being less crowded, you're able to see more of the beauty of the world we live in.

◾ **The guilt of leaving my family**—This is a difficult one. Most people who leave home to travel will experience the feeling of guilt at some point. We have to remember that those we love only want the best for us. They want us to do whatever makes us happy. They would hate to be the reason that's stopped you from taking an amazing opportunity. Remember, you won't be away forever (unless you choose not to come home) and you can go back home at any point if you decide that's what you want. As upsetting as leaving loved ones can be, they will love to see what you get up to on your travels and maybe you'll inspire them to follow in your footsteps.

DO YOU HAVE ANY QUESTIONS
YOU'D LIKE ANSWERED BEFORE YOU GO?

"What does solo travel give you?"

"If you haven't already noticed, I'm addicted to travel. I find it empowering, exhilarating and inspirational. Solo travel has been a necessity for my inner healing and growth. It's brought me opportunities, friendships, answers, curiosity and happiness. Now I've experienced the benefits it's brought to me; I think that travel will always be a part of me and my life."

"Do you have any tips on how to start? Do you plan the locations, then save and book?"

"Yes, decide on your location, do as much research as possible, figure out your budget, save enough money or decide to work while travelling and then book your trip. I go into more detail in the 'Getting Started' chapter."

"How do you budget?"

"The amount of money you'll need to budget will depend on where you're going and how long for. I usually research the costs of the country I plan to visit before I arrive. There are a lot of travel blogs online made by people who have already travelled to your desired country. They'll be able to provide a realistic budget for the destination. I look into the costs of accommodation, flights, local transport, food and any excursions I want to participate in. Then I look at the duration of my trip and add up these costs. Depending on your lifestyle choices, you may need to add on some extra budget."

"How do I find out about coach transfers, nearest banks, nearest airports and laws of a country?"

"Google, Google, Google. Most of this information can be found on Google, but you can ask locals and other tourists as someone usually knows the answer to your question. always speak with other people to find the best way of getting around, as online options can be more expensive. I also find Google Maps helpful as you can type in 'Bank' 'ATM' 'Gym' and available options will pop up. The staff at your accommodation will usually be able to help with information like this. Or check out large online companies like 12go.asia where you can book domestic ferries, buses and trains."

"Who is the best company to book flights with?"

"I usually book my flights through Skyscanner or on an app called Trip.com. If you prefer to book directly with an airline, you can use these sites to search for the cheapest flight and then look on the airline website to find the same option."

"What sparked your ambition?"

"My family. My parents taught me that although money is important to live comfortably, it's important to do what you can to enjoy life and experience as much as possible. My auntie showed me that travelling wherever and whenever you want is possible for anyone, no matter what age you are or what background you come from."

"How did you feel leaving your family? Did you plan to move away entirely?"

"I won't lie, leaving family is the hardest part. Especially when you know you're leaving for a long period, though going away for a short amount of time may just be as difficult if you've never done anything similar before. While I knew I was going to miss them so much, I also felt a lot of guilt about leaving them. This was something I had to work through. From speaking to others on my travels, I learnt that it's extremely common for travellers to feel guilt when leaving their families. The hardest part is saying goodbye at the airport, then after that, these feelings will start to decrease. This time around, I planned to live in Bali, Indonesia for twelve months and then go back home. None of that has gone to plan—I lasted eight months in Bali, travelled around some more countries and now I'm living in Thailand. The twelve-month mark has passed and I'm not sure whether I see myself moving back to the U.K. long-term anytime soon. I love the life I'm living now."

"How do you take care of your health? What about injuries on trips in less-developed countries?"

"There's always a way. There are hospitals and doctors around, even if some may be a few hours' drive away. The locals will help as they know what to do if they're ever in a situation like this themselves. However, we take the free healthcare a lot of us receive in the U.K. for granted, so always ensure you have travel insurance in case of emergencies."

"What's one piece of advice you'd give to yourself if you were starting your travels all over again?"

"Travel with a small hand luggage bag. Seriously, that's the only thing I wish I had done differently when I first started travelling. But for a more detailed answer, I would tell myself to stop worrying, live in the present, say yes to opportunities, don't try to plan too far in advance and enjoy every *single* moment. Solo travel is a rollercoaster, it's an unforgettable experience that we should cherish."

Travel has brought me opportunities, friendships, answers, curiosity and happiness.

@elizacroft_

EXPERIENCES FROM
OTHER FEMALE TRAVELLERS

I have met hundreds of solo travellers, who describe their experience as the "best time of their life." If I haven't already managed to convince you that solo travel could be the best decision you will ever make, I'm hoping that the below experiences from other female travellers might be the tipping point for you to decide you're going to give it a try.

What was one worry you had before going travelling? How did you approach or overcome this?

"The main worry I had was that I was going to get lost. I approached this worry by making sure I had the relevant contact information for people in the local area." —Olivia

"Whether I'd be safe as a female solo traveller was my biggest fear. I overcame this worry by building up my knowledge of all the safety precautions I could take. I also realised that I couldn't use this as an excuse not to travel as there is as much risk of me not being safe in my home town as there is in a different place." —Lucy

"I thought it would be boring without friends, but then I noticed that travelling solo makes it much easier to make new friends and it's not even close to boring." —Gemma

"I was frightened of leaving all the comfort behind and had a fear of leaving a familiar circle. However, I realised that most of what I wanted to do in life involved travel, so I sacrificed life for one year to travel."   —Ian

"I was worried about going through airports on my own, doing it wrong or missing flights but I realised there are so many people and staff in the airports available to help you."   —Michelle

"My main worry was not knowing how I would make new friends when alone. I overcame this by doing as many sociable activities as possible."   —Luke

"My fear was travelling as a single parent with a young child. I approached this by researching child-friendly countries that are safe for female travel. Mostly Asia, they love kids!"   —Kylie

"The worry I had was going on a long flight alone. I approached this by thinking that it's only one to two days out of the many I would spend travelling, I also spent the time focusing on myself."   —Casey

"I had the fear of getting kidnapped. It was scary going somewhere alone for the first time but once I got there and made friends, I felt totally different about it. Most people are *actually really friendly, especially locals in certain countries."*   —Rosanna

"The main worry that I had was being home-sick and feeling alone. I would say, go through it and know it's normal. Also think: what is it that I miss? Is it just the comfort?"   —Mara

"My worry was losing my luggage. I approached this by thinking that it's very unlikely to happen and if it does, I will get it sent to me eventually and in the meantime, I can borrow/buy new things."   —Mia

"The thing I worried about the most was not meeting people with similar interests. I over-came this by participating in activities that I was interested in and I trusted that I will meet similar people by doing this, which I did."   —Jen

How would you describe your overall experience of travelling and do you have any advice for others?

"Empowering."   —Olivia

"Indescribable! You find out who you are and what motivates you in life! It's life-changing. You learn that we take so much for granted. It's a reality check on life's simple but beauti-ful things—like swimming in the sea, sunrises, breathing correctly etc. Exploration is what our bodies crave!"   —Ian

"I feel like such a better person. Travelling improved my mindset massively." —Michelle

"I can't describe the feeling, it was incredible."
—Lucy

"It's the best decision I've ever made. I can't wait to travel again. I love all aspects of travel."
—Kylie

"It changed my life and made me feel more conscious. Adventure is so important."
—Rosanna

"Travelling is the best, when you travel you learn so many new things." —Gemma

"Travel is amazing! You learn so much about yourself. I highly recommend travelling alone."
—Mara

"Magical, I gained so much knowledge about different cultures, myself and life in general."
—Mia

During my travels, I met many amazing women, of all different ages, backgrounds and nationalities, travelling for different reasons. I asked a few of these women to send me a short text to include in this book, explaining their own travel experiences. I'm extremely grateful to have met all these interesting, inspirational women. I'm hoping they will inspire you too.

ROSANNA, 24

How the challenges of solo travel transformed my life

"Travelling has been the most educational thing in my life. It shaped me as a person and enabled me to grow in ways I didn't think possible. Travel opens you up to new cultures and enables you to understand how people live completely different ways of life—some of which are almost impossible to comprehend at first. As someone born and brought up in the U.K., I've realised it can be a very materialistic place, with a culture heavily built around the nine-to-five-life. As other countries take very different approaches, it's liberating to understand different perspectives which you can then take away to decide what you want for yourself.

My biggest learning curves have been when I've travelled alone. This isn't because of the beautiful places I've been to while travelling—I mean yes, they're awesome—but it's actually because of the challenges I've faced along the way. Travelling isn't always rainbows and sunshine, but that is what makes it so important, especially when travelling solo. When I first travelled alone to South East Asia at 19, I arrived at my first destination and cried my eyes out for a whole day because I was so scared. Realising I was eighteen hours away from anyone I cared about and in a foreign country where I didn't understand the culture at all, I felt completely alone and it's honestly one of the scariest feelings I've ever experienced. Because of this, I didn't go outside properly for two days, ate hardly anything and just laid in bed overthinking possible scenarios.

I eventually joined a volunteering group. Fast forward two weeks later, I endured a moment of realisation at how happy life was making me: I had just finished work for the day—I'd been feeding baby sea turtles, preparing for their release the next day. I was sitting with my new group of awesome friends from Belgium and enjoying a beer while watching the sunset—a pure moment of bliss. I realised how all of that upset wasn't just worth it but that it contributed to one of my most valuable times of growth. I so badly wanted to book a flight home and turn away from all this, but had I done that, I'd never be here. And 'here' is the happiest I'd ever felt in my life at that point.

There have been many similar moments like this in the past five years, but now I handle them much better. I recently sold my car, got rid of my flat and all possessions and I carry everything I own in a little backpack. I've got absolutely no clue where my life is heading, but I'm the happiest I've ever been and my soul is free! Humans aren't meant for these intense consumerist social structures, which are designed to keep us in the 'rat-race loop'. We need to be free! Step out of your comfort zone, because it will be hard, yes. You can't expect your life to change if you don't actively do anything to change it."

MARIA, 23
How I Used My Photography Talent To Travel

"Because I'm a documentary and street photographer, I love exploring new places, experiencing new cultures and meeting new people. Through photography, I am inspired by the idea of places, the landscape and how people interact with their homes (concept of psychogeography). Because of this, I always knew that I would be solo travelling at some point in my life. I was very excited to start travelling after college and after the pandemic. I am fascinated by the world and I want to explore it as much as I can while documenting my experiences. I always felt that there must be something more to life than the nine-to-five job, the mortgage and the stereotypical lifestyle that Western society places upon us.

What worried me the most was the fact I was a female solo traveller and the dangers that are associated with that when travelling to third-world countries. Once you are here, you realise that there are so many other people in the exact same boat as you. I also realised that the majority of people you interact with are good and kind people. When you are careful, nothing much will happen to you as a young solo female traveller.

I was also worried that I wouldn't make friends or meet nice people when travelling, but there are so many people travelling solo just like you and it's so easy to meet nice people and make friends. I have more friends here than at home!

I think the more I travel, the more I see the benefits of pushing yourself outside of your comfort zone, meeting new people and having life experiences. As an individual, I feel like my self-worth and self-confidence have grown so much while I've been solo travelling.

Everything in my life has worked out so far for me. I have overcome every obstacle that has been placed on my path, so why would solo travelling be any different?"

MARA, 20
How I Travelled With Homesickness

"I'm Mara, twenty years old and from the Netherlands. In May 2021 I came to Bali: the original plan was that I'd stay for four months to do volunteer work in a school in Ubud. I often experienced homesickness when I was away from home as a kid, so I was nervous about travelling alone (for the first time). I decided to go anyway because of the wanderlust and curiosity in my heart. The travel/flight to Bali was nice, and even during quarantine in Jakarta, things felt very good and exciting! The first few weeks in Bali, however, were tough. I missed home very much and cried a lot. I gave myself three weeks and 'if the feeling was still there', I would allow myself to book a flight back home. And then one day, the homesick feelings were gone. I explored the island, met lovely people, went for walks in beautiful nature and I felt more at home than ever (home in myself)!

It made me realise that it's so important to move through fears and not to make impulsive decisions if you're feeling low. If you face your fears and feel your feelings, things will fall into place and you'll feel so much better!

The volunteer work was great, it's very nice and inspiring to see how grateful the children are. Because I loved Bali so much, I decided to stay longer. I stayed for ten months. It was the best decision I ever made. It taught me a lot about myself (Who am I without all my friends and family? What am I capable of? What do I find important in life? What makes me genuinely happy?). It also taught me a lot about other people and the world in general. When travelling you meet people from all different countries. It's very inspiring to share stories and hear about different cultures.

Travelling gives me a feeling of freedom and lots of inspiration! I love to write and the words flow much more easily if I'm in beautiful new surroundings. I'd recommend anyone to travel alone, or at least to give it a try. Nobody said it was easy... But even in pain (missing people, being confused, stressed, etc), there are some wonderful lessons hidden!

Since being back in the Netherlands, I realise even more how great it was to be abroad for a while. Now I'm trying to integrate all the lessons I've learned into my old environment. It is challenging from time to time, but so freaking worth it!"

KYLIE, 35
How I Travelled The World With A Young Child

"I have been travelling with Frankie since he was a baby. Fun fact, he learnt to walk on his first holiday!

Going further afield, mostly to Asia, was daunting at first, but I never wanted to stop travelling because 1. I was a solo female and 2. I had a young child. My biggest concern, back in 2013, going to Thailand for a month, was what to pack and how I'd manage with luggage, a pushchair and a toddler, all while on a budget! I needn't have worried at all.

Firstly, (almost) everything we have at home in the U.K, you'll find everywhere else in the world too. My first bit of advice is do not overpack, you really don't need as much as you think. Secondly, being alone, you really get out of your comfort zone. I loved meeting new people and asking for help. Most of the time I didn't need to ask. These are some of the friendliest people you'll ever meet. Everyone was happy to help with the baby.

The second bit of advice is to talk to locals as well as other travellers.

Thirdly, travelling in Asia can be as cheap or as expensive as you want it to be. Over the years, we've travelled more and more and for extended periods. The benefits of travelling with a child are honestly priceless. Frankie will sleep anywhere, I'm talking trains, boats, airports...anywhere! You learn to adapt to your surroundings. We have a motto of trying anything/everything once. Frankie doesn't judge a book by its cover—he'll try new foods, play any sports and speak to people he doesn't know. You gain so much confidence from travelling. For me as a single parent and a solo traveller, I've learnt to be open-minded, not to let your doubts get in the way of your dreams and really not to worry about travel, embrace it and enjoy it. I love to travel; I always have and I always will."

ISABEL, 23

I Thought I'd Have To Sacrifice My Career

"I feel so lucky to have made such inspiring friends while travelling and living here in Bali. I think one of the best things about travelling is how easy it is to meet interesting people. My experience of travelling so far has been incredible, but it's been anything but solo. I have a great group of friends in Bali and even though we're all technically travelling solo, I never feel alone or unsupported. It's the best of both worlds knowing that I have the ultimate freedom of travelling by myself, but if I find myself stuck or needing good company, a friend is never far. Before I left Ireland, I think I was most afraid of missing out on building a career. I was worried that my peers would turn me out when I quit my job, that I would be left out and left behind. I always knew it was a sacrifice I was willing to make, but I never guessed how amazing it would be and how many doors it would open. The longer I spend living with this choice, the happier I am that I made it. Nothing compares to the freedom I have now and I couldn't imagine giving it up any time soon. Each day in Bali has brought another new experience and it makes me realise how crazy I was to assume I would be missing out if I went travelling! I am so excited to keep exploring, gathering experiences and seeing the world. I wouldn't change a thing."

SARAH, 27

How My First Travel Experience Led Me To Living In Australia

"I first got the idea to travel when I met my flatmate, Lauren. Lauren really vouched that what I truly needed was to go move abroad and see the world. But I had doubts about whether I could really go off and do this on my own. I didn't believe I was sensible enough to make the right decisions to keep myself safe. I started off by travelling to Thailand on a group tour. This way I had the security of knowing that someone reputable and safe was meeting me on the other side. I also had a sense of security by meeting a group—I wouldn't feel alone and I could rely on trustworthy guides to take me to all the best places. That took away the challenge of planning where to go and what to do to use my time wisely out of the equation. I did a few similar adventures, meeting groups to travel to Bali and then Costa Rica. Thanks to these experiences, I knew that travel was for me and made me happy, so I took the plunge to move to Australia. Australia challenged me to put myself out there and join social groups to make friends. I started bodyweight training and fell in love with the journey, making solid friendships along the way. These long-term friends and deep connections then led me to become a qualified yoga instructor. When travelling, you meet people who are fiercely independent and successful, because they do not let fear hold them back, and they follow their own path and inspire you to find yours and do the same. I am truly grateful to have met Eliza in Bali, who has continued to inspire me in my business ventures and to uphold the confidence of believing in yourself and spreading your wings to see the world. Travelling lets us work on stepping outside our comfort zone, which then challenges the limiting beliefs in our mindset that hold us back. With a stronger mindset, it's no wonder the people who travel go on to achieve great things. In life, we are always going to be faced with fears and doubts, most of which are irrational and never come true. But what's worse, listening to the fear in our heads? Or listening to the voice when we are eighty, saying damn, I wish I had done that, I regret not taking that leap? You only have one life, now is the time to live it. Catch the flight, see where it takes you, and don't look back. The world is full of opportunities, but you have to put yourself out there to go and find them."

BETH, 23
How I Did It During University

"My travelling experience is centred around the summer of 2019 when I went inter-railing with my best friend from university. We visited nine cities across five countries, starting in Berlin in Germany and travelling down to Hvar, just off the coast of Split in Croatia. It was one of the best times of my life, meeting new people, experiencing new cultures and making new memories.

I was so excited to go away and explore so many new cities. The longest we stayed in one place was three nights, so packing in excursions and the sights was a top priority. We stayed in hostels, bar maybe one Airbnb, which meant meeting people was relatively easy (this was a concern for me prior to travelling). Many people are in the same situation as you, travelling alone or in a small group and are eager to make new friends. We made friends on our first night of the trip. Our new acquaintances were doing a very similar route to us, which meant we could meet up again in a couple of weeks and they introduced us to a new city we hadn't initially considered visiting.

The excitement can sometimes be tainted by the unknown of new places and the associated risks, mainly those you hear about on social media. In general, my worries were the same as in the U.K., being out late at night and being unfamiliar with my surroundings and not having the comfort blanket of being close to home and family. To overcome this required mainly to have your wits about you. There are multiple people doing as you are who are kind and helpful, be careful and check in with loved ones and friends as often as you can, not only to ease their minds. I am sure they would love to see you living your best life too!

Travelling gives you a new sense of freedom, which is different to going to university and living away from home. You are experiencing different people, cultures, cities and cuisines. I found it pushed me out of my comfort zone in a way I had never been pushed before, and I cannot wait to go travelling again in the near future. South East Asia is the next stop!"

MAXINE, 51
How I Did It With Little Support

"There weren't a lot of options for foreign travel in the 70s and early 80s. There was no Internet or Google, no budget airlines or Airbnb or any of the things that make travel so much easier and more affordable today. Even travel to Spain, France and Greece was expensive and places like Prague, Budapest and Dubrovnik which have huge tourism industries now, were behind the iron curtain and closed to western travellers.

As someone whose family holidays rarely included any highlights, the furthest I'd been from home in Lancashire up to age fourteen was a wet week in a caravan in Cornwall and two school water sports holidays to the south of France via a 24-hour coach trip!

While at college, I finally saved up to go on a holiday that included an aeroplane! It was not a memorable experience apart from someone dying due to falling from a balcony while drunk and the thought of doing a similar holiday again did not appeal to me.

I've always been an independent spirit and the two-week blowout drinking holidays were not for me! I wanted to see the world but with travel so expensive I focused on earning money and establishing a career after graduating from university in 1992.

I got the travel bug in my mid-twenties. I'd graduated university and started a full-time job, bought my first house and slowly started to build up savings to be able to travel more. I had a friend from school who had gone to live and work first in the States and then in Canada and a chance meeting with her mum led to reconnection and organising a trip to go to visit her in Toronto. That started a lifelong love affair with Canada, which is still going strong thirty-five years later.

I loved everything about Toronto even though it was minus 20 degrees in February and I didn't have appropriate clothing! The first trip to Niagara Falls, the view from CN Tower, the baseball stadium called the Rogers Centre (formerly the Sky-Dome) with its retractable roof, the shores of Lake Ontario—it was all so far removed from a wet weekend in Blackpool.

In my late twenties, I had a decent job and disposable income for travel and I was single. But I found a lot of my friends had either gotten married and had kids or they didn't have any money to travel to the places I wanted to visit!

In the summer of 1996, after the breakdown of my most recent relationship, I had I rang a friend who was working with British Airways on a whim, and said, "Where can I go this weekend?"

She had access to cheap BA flights which she could book on my behalf. The list came out early in the week for places where not many seats had been sold. I can't remember all the places that week, but one that came up was Prague and it was £79 to fly via Heathrow, so I said, "Book it!"

I knew nothing about Prague, but it sounded more exciting than a trip to Magaluf or Benidorm.

I packed a bag with some clothes for the weekend and got on the plane for my first-ever solo trip. I hadn't booked any accommodation as I assumed I could do that at the airport. In those days most airports had a help desk where you could organise a hotel and transfers. I've always been a 'something always turns up' kind of person and not one to stress about needing to know exactly where I was going or staying. I thought, Prague is a city, so how hard can it be?

Well, apparently finding a hotel in Prague in July 1996 was very difficult! There was no 'help desk' at the airport. Having not long been a democracy after the fall of communism, the tourism industry was still in its infancy. There were no mobile phones, Google didn't exist nor did anything like Expedia hotels, Airbnb or booking.com.

I still smoked in those days, so my first priority when I arrived anywhere was to get outside and have a smoke! As I sat on a bench in the summer sunshine, I was feeling pretty pleased with myself and the excitement of the unknown. I got chatting to a fellow smoker from Ireland and asked if he could recommend a hotel in Prague on account of the non-help-desk at the airport. His response took me a bit by surprise as his first words were, "You haven't booked anything?" He then explained that I'd probably struggle to find anything as it was summer, but he told me to try around Wenceslas Square as he seemed to think there were some hotels there. I finished my cigarette and headed for the taxi rank. The drivers spoke no English but Wenceslas Square seemed to register so off we went!

By the time I arrived in Wenceslas Square, it was early evening and I walked into the first hotel I found to see if they had a room available. I was told they were fully booked. After the fourth try, I was running out of hotels and started to regret not doing a little bit more planning! It was getting dark and the area I was in seemed to double as the red-light district! I asked the receptionist at the last option if they could help me as I explained I'd just arrived and needed a place to stay for four nights and didn't want to keep walking in the dark on my own. The very helpful person said they could get me a room at the Hotel Paris but it was £200 for one night, which was way over the £50 per night budget I had set myself. As they say, beggars can't be choosers so I accepted the offer and she called me a taxi to take me there. After a very expensive 45-minute taxi ride (it felt like taxis were run by the local mafia in 1996), I arrived at the hotel and paid for the one night and said I'd let them know the next day if I was staying longer. The Hotel Paris was the fanciest hotel I'd ever stayed in, but I was happy to have found a room and after a quick drink and snacks in the bar, I headed to bed with the sole intent of finding a cheaper hotel in the morning when daylight arrived!

In the morning I woke up starving. I got up early and headed out to see where the hell I was! I walked down a few narrow streets looking for hotel signs and suddenly found myself in the most beautiful square I had ever seen—three amazing churches, amazing carved buildings, a statue of someone and some restaurants with patios. I sat down and a waiter came and gave me a menu which was in Czech. There was not an English translation in sight. Not wanting to cause a fuss and given that the waiter spoke very little English together with my zero Czech, I ended up pointing at the food the people on the table next to me were eating along with the word cappuccino as apparently, that word is universal!

As I drank my coffee in the morning sun, people-watching with church bells ringing in this beautiful square, I felt calm and happy soaking up the moment. I didn't take any photos and I have nothing captured on a phone, yet I can still remember the feeling of being in that square at that moment twenty-five years later!

I finished my coffee and walked around the streets on the edge of the square as I definitely wanted to stay in this area. As luck would have it, I stumbled across a sign that said 'Hotel Central.' It was no Hotel Paris but it was £45 per night and they had rooms so I booked for the three nights I had left, collected my bag from Hotel Paris, downgraded my sleeping arrangements, picked up a city map and looked forward to discovering what else the city had to offer!"

Travel Blogger & TV Host JAMIE BANKS
Why I Think You Should Go For It

"I started travelling solo because I wanted to travel often, and I wasn't going to wait around for someone to come with me. It was hard to find someone with an aligned schedule, or just someone who wanted to travel as much as me, so I just went by myself. I have been to twenty-five countries, mostly solo.

There used to be times when I felt nervous before a solo trip. This was especially the case if a place was considered not incredibly 'safe', by people's perceptions, the media, and legitimate statistics. But I just went anyway. We must get out of our comfort zone. It is more comfortable for me to sit and relax all day and watch Netflix in a warm bed. Sometimes travel is uncomfortable—long journeys, early mornings, motion sickness, stomach issues, it is not always easy. But staying inside in one place is not what brings me adventure or joy.

If you are considering solo travel, I say do it. If you feel a calling in your heart to see new places, and have more adventures, it is because it is possible for you. You want more out of your life, and you have to honour that.

Don't wait around for someone else to start living the life of your dreams. Start now. You don't have to wait for the 'perfect' opportunity. It probably will never come. Book one trip and see how it goes. You can choose somewhere close or far, somewhere familiar or somewhere you have always desired to visit.

One day you will look back on your life. What do you think you will remember fondly and what will you regret? The adventures you had? Or the things you wanted to do and didn't because you were too nervous, tired, lazy, or just never found the right time?

Start living the life that you have imagined."

"Through travel I first became aware of the outside world; it was through travel that I found my own introspective way into becoming a part of it."

Eudora Welty—Novelist

If you feel called in your heart to see new places and have more adventures, it's because it is possible for you.

@jamiebanks_

THE FINAL &
MOST IMPORTANT TIP

If you're thinking about it, GO FOR IT—give it a try and see how it benefits your life and you as an individual. You will never regret trying, but you will always regret *not* trying. In a previous chapter, I talked about finding your 'why?' but you should also ask yourself 'why not?'. Why not go for it? If it's always on your mind, the world is calling you, this is meant for you.

Your life does not need to feel figured out right now. Solo travel is a great way to distance yourself from all the familiarities, cut out all distractions and figure your journey out by yourself without experiencing subliminal societal pressures and the pressures from those around you. Your life is yours alone and if you try to do the 'right' thing, then you'll end up following someone else's vision instead of your own. Solo travel is about transformation, courage and a lust for adventure and experience.

Taking the leap may feel risky, but the bigger risk is taking no action on the desires you have because you'll only be living a life that isn't aligned with your passions. I noticed that once I took the first risk, I had less fear of taking the next risk, because I found that everything worked out the first time. Everything always works out, even if it's not in the way you expected it to be.

Think about it strategically, but don't think about it for too long, otherwise you might let your fears stop you, or excuses will start to creep in. What habits do you need to develop and which ones do you need to break? Are there any sacrifices you need to make? Which people do you need to surround yourself with? Are there any skills you need to learn? What's the first step you need to take? Stride past your fears, make a plan and go for it. Amazing things will start to happen, don't be scared of *living*!

Imagine if you never take a chance on your dream. How much would you regret it? You don't want to be asking yourself what kind of life you could have created if you'd just taken the chance. The unknown future might be better than you could ever imagine it to be. Instead of thinking about what could go wrong, you should always be optimistic and think about all the things that could go right and all the opportunities that may arise from this decision. Don't waste your potential, go through the transition period to discover who you are and watch yourself emerge into your best self. Solo travel is an enriching experience, it gives you a constant feeling of being truly alive in your stomach.

You've already overcome every other challenge life has thrown at you, what makes you think you won't be able to deal with this one too? Regardless of your circumstances, be bold and brave, trust in yourself and embark on the journey. Your desire alone should be enough of a reason for you to take the leap. You deserve to chase those wild dreams of yours.

I hope I've inspired you to go and explore the world. Travelling may be the best decision you ever make. I'm incredibly excited for more of you to experience solo travel. Get out there and see the world, girls!

GO
FOR
IT

@elizacroft_

ACKNOWLEDGEMENTS

This book would not have been possible without my family. You have given me so much unconditional love and support throughout my life.

I would like to thank my friends and everyone I've met during my travels. Your inspiration and encouragement haven't gone unnoticed.

Lastly, a big thank you to Brian Gruber and Tom Vater for your help and guidance with publishing this book.

LET'S CONNECT!

I'd love to know if this book has inspired you to take the leap. Let's connect on socials!

Follow my travel journey on Instagram — elizacroft_

Follow my TikTok for all my latest solo travel tips — paradisetravels_

Made in United States
North Haven, CT
26 June 2023

38248561R00124